Memoirs of a Woman from Bialystok (Białystok, Poland)

Translation of

ZIKHROYNES FUN A BIALYSTOKER FROY

Author: Rachel Anna Kositza

Originally published in Los Angeles, 1964

A Publication of JewishGen, Inc.
Edmond J. Safra Plaza, 36 Battery Place, New York, NY 10280
646.494.2972 | info@JewishGen.org | www.jewishgen.org

Memoirs of a Woman from Bialystok (Białystok, Poland)
Translation of *Zikhroynes Fun A Bialystoker Froy*

Author: Rachel Anna Kositza
Project Coordinator: Susan Kingsley Pasquariella
Translated by: Beate Schützmann-Krebs
Extraction of English text: Donni Magid
Cover Design: Rachel Kolokoff Hopper
Layout: Jonathan Wind

Library of Congress Control Number (LCCN): 2023949792

ISBN: 978-1-954176-89-8 (hard cover: 200 pages, alk. paper)

About JewishGen.org

JewishGen, an affiliate of the Museum of Jewish Heritage - A Living Memorial to the Holocaust, serves as the global home for Jewish genealogy.

Featuring unparalleled access to 30+ million records, it offers unique search tools, along with opportunities for researchers to connect with others who share similar interests. Award winning resources such as the Family Finder, Discussion Groups, and ViewMate, are relied upon by thousands each day.

In addition, JewishGen's extensive informational, educational and historical offerings, such as the Jewish Communities Database, Yizkor Book translations, InfoFiles, Family Tree of the Jewish People, and KehilaLinks, provide critical insights, first-hand accounts, and context about Jewish communal and familial life throughout the world.

Offered as a free resource, JewishGen.org has facilitated thousands of family connections and success stories, and is currently engaged in an intensive expansion effort that will bring many more records, tools, and resources to its collections.

Please visit https://www.jewishgen.org/ to learn more.

Executive Director: Avraham Groll

About JewishGen Press

JewishGen Press (formerly the Yizkor Books-in-Print Project) is the publishing division of JewishGen.org, and provides a venue for the publication of non-fiction books pertaining to Jewish genealogy, history, culture, and heritage.

In addition to the Yizkor Book category, publications in the Other Non-Fiction category include Shoah memoirs and research, genealogical research, collections of genealogical and historical materials, biographies, diaries and letters, studies of Jewish experience and cultural life in the past, academic theses, and other books of interest to the Jewish community.

Please visit https://www.jewishgen.org/Yizkor/ybip.html to learn more.

Director of JewishGen Press: Joel Alpert
Managing Editor - Jessica Feinstein
Publications Manager - Susan Rosin

Notes to the Reader

The original book can be seen online at the Yiddish Book Center website:

https://www.yiddishbookcenter.org/collections/yiddish-books/spb-nybc209738/kositza-rachel-anna-zikhroynes-fun-a-byalistoker-froy

The Yiddish title of this book has been transcribed according to the internationally recognized YIVO standard [YIVO: Yidisher Visnshaftlekher Institut]. The original title of the book is: "Zichroines Fun A Bialystoker Froi".

A list of all books available from JewishGen Press along with prices is available at:
https://www.jewishgen.org/Yizkor/ybip.html

Preface and Dedication of the Translator

Rachel Anna Grutski is not only pretty, creative and hardworking, but also a very self-assured and independent girl for her time. Her life was never easy. Born in 1868 in the Jewish colony of Zakova (kolonja Izaaka/Isaaka/Izakova), not far from Bialystok and Grodno, Rachel had to toil hard to help provide for the family's livelihood. Even as a very young child, she worked long hours in her family's household and agricultural fields, in a matzo bakery, and later in the Bialystok textile factories.

She describes the Jewish daily life and history of the colony, the economic and personal challenges she, her family members and neighbours face, and she details the plight of the Bialystok factory workers and the world of Bialystok's richest factory owners.

Rachel is touchingly devoted to her family and musters almost superhuman strength for them, working her way up in the factories with cleverness, skill, and incredible diligence, and develops survival skills and wisdom in the face of ever-changing problems and difficulties.

We walk through the streets of Bialystok with Rachel and meet her colleagues, friends and later husband, Avrom Itskhok Kositza, who lives in the city's poor district. Despite setbacks and hardships, the small Kositza family grows and faces new challenges with determination, experiencing small victories along the way.

A deep shock is left by the Bialystok pogrom of 1905, which Rachel and her family barely survive. But finally, Rachel sees no future in her homeland and emigrates to America in 1906, where her life story continues...

I dedicate this translation to Tomek Wisniewski for the opening of his smallest Jewish museum in the world in Bialystok, "The Place", Memoirs of a Woman from Bialystok translated from Yiddish - Społeczne Muzeum Żydów Białegostoku i regionu (jewishbialystok.pl)

My heartfelt thanks to my dear friend, **Susan Pasquariella**, who proofread my English translation with love and patience and shares my great emotion and enthusiasm for Rachel Anna Kositza and her memoirs. Special thanks to Rachel Kositza's family, Dr. Norton Snyder and Mark Snyder and to my friends, Joanna Czaban, Rabbi Irwin Keller and Michael Cohen.

Beate Schützmann-Krebs
July 2023

Photo Credits

Front Cover:
Rachel Anna Kositza, born Grutski, writing her book, photo courtesy of her grandson, Dr. Norton Snyder (page 2).

Back Cover
Upper Left: *Grodno, old card,* courtesy of Dr. Tomek Wisniewski (page 7).
Lower Right: *(Possibly) Rachel with her three daughters,* photo courtesy of her grandson, Dr. Norton Snyder (page 122)

Front and back cover background digital illustration by Rachel Kolokoff Hopper.

Geopolitical Information

Białystok, Poland is located at 53°08' N 23°09' E and 109 miles NE of Warszaw

	Town	District	Province	Country
Before WWI (c. 1900):	Belostok	Białystok	Grodno	Russian Empire
Between the wars:	Białystok	Białystok	Białystok	Poland
After WWII (c. 1950):	Białystok			Poland
Today (c. 2000):	Białystok			Poland

Alternate Names for the Town:

Białystok [Pol], Byalistok [Yid], Belostok [Rus], Belastok [Bel], Balstogė [Lith], Bjalistoka [Latv], Bialistok, Bielastok

Nearby Jewish Communities:

Wasilków 5 miles NNE

Choroszcz 7 miles W

Supraśl 10 miles NE

Zabłudów 12 miles SE

Suraż 15 miles SSW

Łapy 16 miles SW

Tykocin 16 miles WNW

Knyszyn 16 miles NW

Jasionówka 18 miles NNW

Michałowo 20 miles ESE

Zawady 21 miles W

Narew 21 miles SE

Sokoły 21 miles WSW

Gródek 22 miles E

Korycin 22 miles N

Janów Sokolski 23 miles N

Trzcianne 24 miles NW

Sokółka 24 miles NE

Bielsk Podlaski 25 miles S

Krynki 28 miles ENE

Goniądz 29 miles NW

Rutki 30 miles W

Wysokie Mazowieckie 30 miles WSW

Brańsk 30 miles SSW

Jewish Population: 47,783 (in 1895), 44,940 (in 1939)

POLAND – CURRENT BORDERS

Map of Poland showing the location of **Białystok**

Memoirs of a Woman from Bialystok
(Białystok, Poland)

53°08' / 23°09'

Translation of:
Zikhroynes fun a Bialystoker Froy

Author: Rachel Anna Kositza

Originally published in Los Angeles, 1964

Acknowledgments

Project Coordinator:

Susan Kingsley Pasquariella

Translator:

Beate Schützmann-Krebs

Our sincere appreciation to Susan Kingsley Pasquariella and Beate Schützmann-Krebs, for their permission to put this material on the JewishGen web site.

The original book may be viewed at the Yiddish Book Center.

We wish to thank Donni Magid for extracting the English translation, enabling this online presentation.

This is a translation of: *Zikhroynes fun a Bialystoker Froy*
Memoirs of a Woman from Bialystok,
Author: Rachel Anna Kositza. Originally published in Los Angeles,
1964

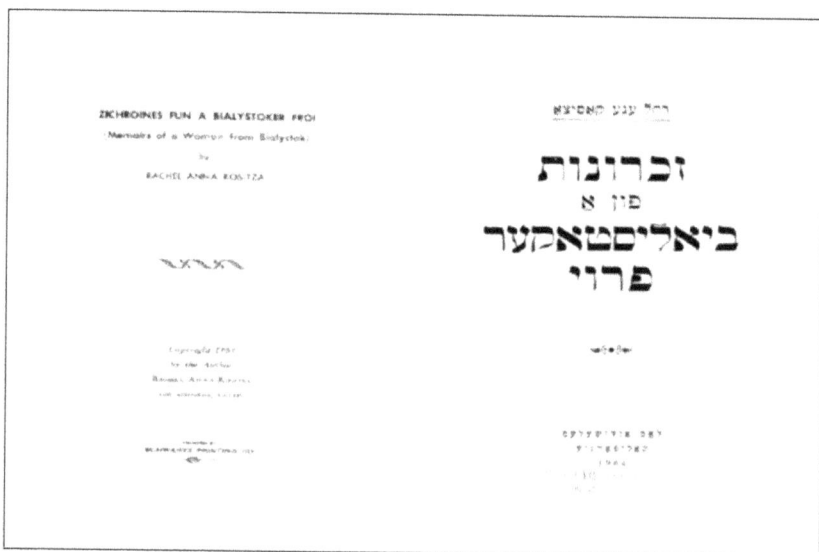

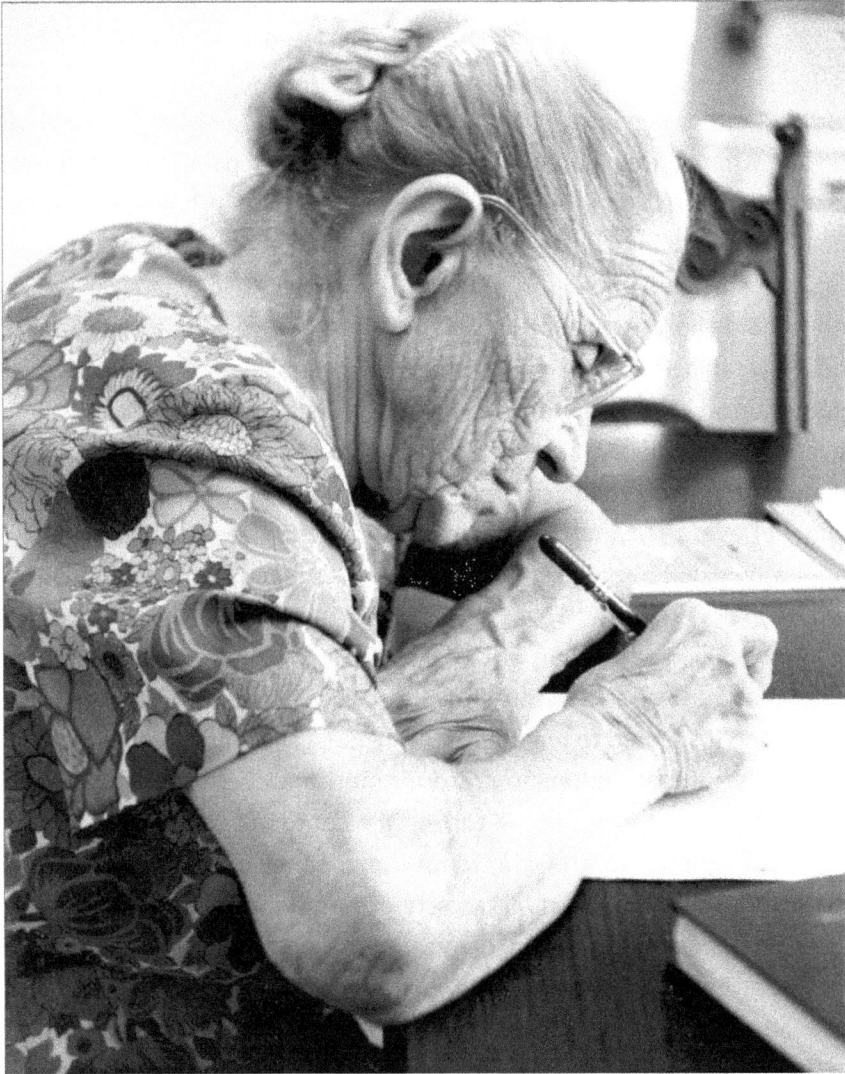

Rachel Anna Kositza, writing her book,
photo courtesy of her grandson,
Dr. Norton Snyder

Memoirs of a Woman from Bialystok

FOREWORD

My mother began to write her memoirs at the age of eighty six. It all began when I told her about Grandma Moses' painting career and challenged her to do likewise. Never one to pass up a challenge, but not being able to paint, she decided to try her hand at writing.

And so, every day, for a period of almost two years, after her household chores were completed (this included cooking for her family, house cleaning and gardening), she would set aside an hour or two for her writing. I can see her now so clearly, sitting at the kitchen table, bent over her white-lined paper, writing away in her round, even, measured handwriting, and proudly showing me each neatly written page, and then with her ever-ready humor, looking up at me, her face broadening into a grin, a twinkle in her light blue eyes, and laughing: "I am now indeed a writer."

And as she kept at her writing and finally finished the book, I never ceased to marvel at her self-discipline, her singleness of purpose, her drive. And it seemed to me that in this respect she was representative of a type that is fast disappearing from American Jewish life – the Jewish immigrant woman who at the turn of the century, came out of the East European ghetto to the ghetto of America, and by sheer grit and perseverance, undeterred by poverty or hard work, opened up for her children opportunities for the highest education and self development.

The grit and perseverance exemplified by my mother was nurtured by the colonyeh. The Jewish colonyeh of Czarist times was an agrarian settlement about which little has been written. The Jews who lived there farmed the land and raised livestock and were authentic peasants.

I am sure that many readers of this book will see in it not only my mother, but their mothers as well, and will remember proudly their origins, back-ground, and the strength and courage of their forebears.

G.R. 1977

(Page 5)

1.

My grandfather was called *Abraham Grutski* of Zubritz; he was my father's father...

I can't have any memories of it, but I think it happened 152 years ago, namely when the Tsar in Russia issued a decree that Jews should be driven out of the villages. My grandfather also lived in a village called Zubritz, so he too was driven out...

A vyorst [0.66 miles] from the village, they founded a colony, where also my grandpa settled, because he did not know where else he could have gone. He had a large family, a wife and six children, three sons and three daughters. One was named *Blumke*, the second *Gitl* and the third *Sheyne*. The eldest son was named *Shmuel*, the second was my father, his name was *Leybe*, and the third son was named *Mendl*. He died very young. That was told to me by my parents...

In the colony were allocated fields, the amount of which was based on the size of the family, that is, the number of sons in a family. Daughters were not included in the calculation. Since my grandfather had three sons, he got a registry and half a country estate [1]. My father and his brothers worked in the fields, plowing and sowing. But when they were grown up and had weddings, each one got part of his [grandpa's] fields.

That was the law. The fields were divided into many parts by the colony. In one part rye and wheat were sown, on another barley or potatoes; on still another peas, lentils and buckwheat. One of these parts measured about two vyorst [2,1 km].

The rye and wheat had to be sown before Sukkot, because it needed to warm up before winter and started to grow after Passover. In the second yearit was not allowed to sow the rye and wheat in the same field. The field had to remain fallow for a whole year, nothing was sown on it, only the cattle pastured there on the grass ...

---

[1] literally "field", farm land

(Page 6)

After Passover, barley, potatoes, peas, lentils and buckwheat were sown. Barley and potatoes had to be sown in suitable places so that they did not burn. The same was true for oats, lentils and peas. The buckwheat was sown on the mountains.

Downstairs at the house people used to have a garden. Here grew cucumbers, beets, carrots, turnips, large and small beans, pumpkins, Turkish wheat and all kinds of vegetables.

It was necessary to keep cows, oxen and horses. The cows gave milk, and from the milk they made butter and cheese. The family ate it, but part of it was also sold in the surrounding towns. The oxen were used for tilling the fields, the horses were used for plowing and sowing, or they were used to go to town to buy what was needed for the colony. Those who did not own a horse took the ox in its place for all these activities...

After my grandfather's first wife died, he married a second wife with whom he had two sons: one was named *Artsik* [or Artshik] the second *Yerakhmiel* [or Rakhmiel]. The family grew larger and soon had no livelihood. So the daughters moved to other cities as maids and saved money as dowries, because without dowries the girls could not marry. The sons fared better. They received a dowry and also got a share of the fields that their grandfather owned...

I remember Grandpa. At that time I was still a little girl, about 8 years old. He wasn't tall, but he had a long beard. I remember how he died. It happened near the colony, in a small town called Amdur. Grandfather was leading a young cow there and wanted to sell it, but the cow became wild and robbed him of his strength. He fell down in the market and had a vein burst. He was taken home, but it was not long before he died. He lived to be seventy-two years old. I was no older than twelve at the time. Today, as I write about it, I am already eighty-six years old...

The colony[1] was located two miles from Sokółka, two miles from Kuznitse [Kuźnica], about twelve miles from Amdur, four miles from Grodno

---

[1] Find more about this colony [colony Zakova, also called Izakova, Isaaka] here:

https://kehilalinks.jewishgen.org/kolonja/colonists.html?fbclid=IwAR19xHSTY rM5 BiBdnf3PxOHjwOf4yNSj8_ApxuzJStOpc1bhxfLn_-qgRcs

(Page 7)

and fifteen miles from Bialystok. The address was written: Grodner gubernye [provincial government], Sokolovskovo district, Zakova [Żakowo] colony.

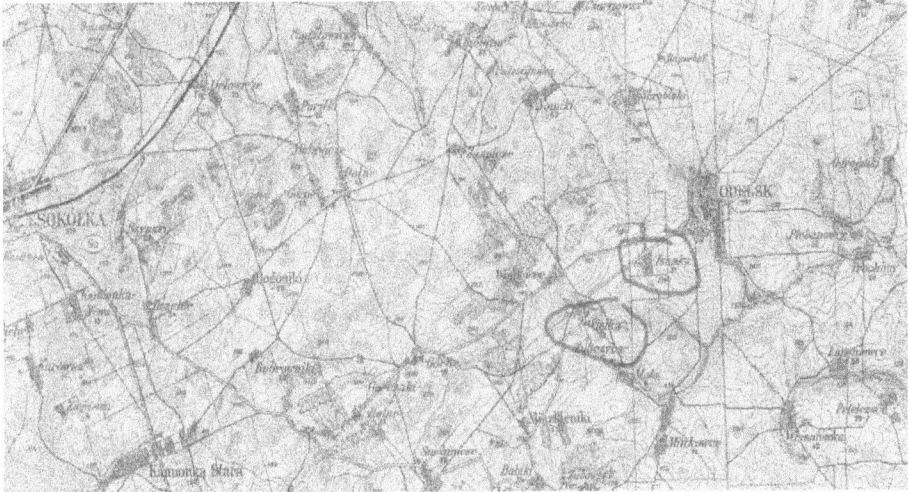

Old map: courtesy of Dr.Tomek Wisniewski, colony Isaaka (Izakova, Zakova), Wielka Zubrzyca (Zubritz), Odelsk and Sokółka

Grodno, old photograph, courtesy of Dr. Tomek Wisniewski

Grodno, old card, courtesy of Dr. Tomek Wisniewski

Grodno, old card, courtesy of Dr. Tomek Wisniewski

2.

My great-grandfather's name was *Yeshue Dubrovski*. He was my mother's grandfather and also lived in a village. When the Tsar issued the decree that no more Jews were allowed to live in the villages, he moved to Grodno. He bought horse-drawn carts and hired workers to bring and sell water, because there were no wells in Grodno. So the families had to buy water from the water carriers. As my mother told me, the earnings were not bad. My mother grew up with him; when her mother died, she was only two years old. And when my mother's father died, she was just four. Her grandfather was very good to her, and her grandmother even better.

My mother's father was called Reb *Abraham Ber* and was ordained as a rabbi. This was told to me by my mother, who in turn was told it by her mother, and she also told me what life was like at that time. She always used to speak about her father. She had never seen him, but she was told that he had died in tallith and tefillin, in the Pinsk Bes-Medresh [Beth Midrash], where he studied...

But now I want to tell you what my mother told me about her

upbringing. Her grandfather taught her the Hebrew script and instructed her in the Pentateuch. She also went to the kheyder [cheder]. Later, when she was older, her grandfather gave her to a seamstress so that she could learn the trade and later earn a living with it.

My mother had a twin sister, but an uncle took her and raised her. He was called *Khone Dvoyre's [Deborah's]*. Actually, there were three uncles who had the same fate as all the village people; they were driven out of the villages and they went around to find an income opportunity somewhere else. One settled in Kershits, the second in Shanbel, and the third, who

(Page 8)

raised my mother's sister in his home, settled in Yekaterinodar (Krasnodar). There my mother's sister studied at the high school. She married a pharmacist, what in America is called a druggist. My aunt did not know that she left a sister in Grodno, because when my uncle took her to raise her, she was only two years old. When my aunt was already forty years old, she learned that she had left a sister behind in Grodno. She sent a letter to friends in Grodno, and they gave it to my mother. Now you can imagine how great her joy was!

From then on, the twin sisters began to write letters to each other. My aunt wrote that she was rich, her husband had died and she had become a widow. At that time, my mother was also already a widow, but very poor. That's why my aunt asked if it wouldn't be a good plan if I came to her in Krasnodar; she wanted to send money so that I could come to her. But when I was ready to go, something happened so I couldn't leave. After that, my mother lost her sister's address and they stopped writing to each other.

This happened 67 years ago. After that we heard that the Jews were driven out of deep Russia and there were pogroms there. We don't know what happened to my aunt and her family, and so my mother was separated from her sister forever.

3.

Now I want to tell you what happened to the child of my great-grandfather, *Yeshue Dubrovski*:

Just as the world does not remember, surely everyone has already forgotten what happened 120 years back in Russia, while Nicholas the First was ruling. He issued a decree, that is, a punitive action on Jews, that Jewish parents should be deprived of their young boys as soldiers. They had to serve for a whole 25 years.

(Page 9)

The older boys hid in the woods, but the four-year-old boys were unable to hide in the woods, so people used to come at night and drag them out of their beds. This is what happened at my mother's grandfather's house. They came in the middle of the night and stole his four-year-old child forever, never to be heard from again, he had disappeared from the face of the earth...The Russian murderers drove the children into a river and "baptized" them...some survived, and others died.

In the narrative of humanity this has already been forgotten, but I think it is necessary to tell it to my children and in front of the whole world, to all who read this. But now I come to the main thing: a miracle occurred to the Jews. Once the Tsar, Nicholas the Second, was riding at night with his aides in a horse-drawn carriage beside a river. Suddenly the horses stopped and refused to move from the place. [The Tsar] lifts his head and sees a man standing in the river, but the river is made of blood, and the man cannot get out of the blood. Then he asks his generals what this means. They answer that they had to think about this. They consulted and then told him to take back the decree on the Jews and not to take any more little Jewish children as soldiers. He did so, and when he came to the river the second time, he no longer saw anyone there. He was told that the person he saw in the river was his grandfather Nicholas. Nicholas changed the decree. No more young children were to be conscripted, and military service was limited to six years. Adult boys of 21 years of age have since been taken. However, if they were drafted at 21, they also had to suffer. They were usually sent to Siberia in the cold provinces, and I still remember how the parents suffered. You can imagine how it was then, because there were no railroads yet. [The conscripted boys] were driven from one town to another and from one province to another, while the snow reached their arms and the frost was very strong. Not all the soldiers endured this; some died and others came home sick...

All of this took place in Russia. We in America today don't know about these things and have no idea what our parents had to suffer...

(Page 10)

4.

When my mother's grandfather died, she was ten years old, could already sew well and earned one ruble a week. But it was not enough for her living. Her uncle, her father's brother, who was called Velvel the Bezdetnik [the Childless], because he had no children, was a very good man. He took care that my mother did not lack food. His wife, however, was very bad, and when my mother came from work to her uncle's house, but he was not at home, she remained hungry.

My mother lived in a suburb of Grodno. To get to work, she had to go to the city every day, across the river Nyeman [Neman]. To do that, you had to take a boat; in the summer it was fine, but in the winter it was dangerous. The ice had to be chopped up to get into the city. This was a hard life for my parentless mother. She had to stay with family members, sometimes with an uncle and sometimes with an aunt. Her uncle, Velvel the Bezdetnik was from her father's side. In the suburb she also had a rich and distinguished aunt who had her own ship that regularly sailed across the Neman. She was her mother's sister and her name was Khaye-Feyge. However, my mother could not go to her because she had two daughters who were jealous of my mother for being very pretty. One girl was named Rive-Leye and the second Teybl. Both girls quarreled with my mother. So you can imagine how she suffered...Rive-Leye was rich, unlike Teybl. When I grew older, I used to visit them in Grodno. Many times I was at Rive-Leye's, she welcomed me very warmly...

Later I heard that she was in America with her family. She had four sons. One of the sons had a wife and children who drowned on the ship "Titanic"...

5.

My father was called *Leybe Grutske [Grutski]*. He was born in 1844 and died in 1893, that is, very young. My father

(Page 11)

was an educated man. He could write very beautifully in Yiddish and also very well in Hebrew. He was able to study Torah portions, Rashi and Gemara, and to lead congregational prayers. Once he studied the Mishna, as I saw myself, with the Jews in the Bes-Hamedresh [Beth ha-Midrash]...

When his mother died, he was about six years old. She died very young. How old she was I don't know, only that they called her Rachel. I, the author of this story, am named after her. My father worked very hard in the fields, and there was no joy in the house either. There were always quarrels with the stepmother...

As my father grew older, he began to think about starting his own family. In the colony there was a beautiful girl named *Khaye*. She used to join him in the field where he was working. They were related to each other; her brother, *Moyshe Zeliks*, was married to my sister *Sheyne* [1]. But nothing came of my father's love. She couldn't wait, and when a young man came from Krynki, they got married. However, she did not become happy with him and divorced him...

My father began to look for a bride outside the colony, because none of the girls there appealed to him. He himself was handsome and healthy, broad-shouldered but not fat, a hero of a man; a blond with beautiful blue eyes...When he used to shout at the "meshshtanes" [the more privileged citizens] who came to the Jewish fields with their cattle, it was enough that they heard his voice to flee immediately, as if a fire had broken out...Matchmakers began to visit him and proposed a matrimonial union, namely a wedding in Grodno. Grodno was about four miles from the colony. My grandpa and my father went to Grodno with the matchmaker to meet a beautiful girl who actually became my father's bride.

She was said to be no good for the colony, because in the colony you had to work hard in the fields. In summer, the grain had to be cut, rye, wheat, barley, oats and others. One had to cultivate, sow, thresh, cut, dig, and the women helped the men. My mother did not want

---

[1] I think this is typo and it must be **his** sister Sheyne.

(Page 12)

this wedding at all. She said that she could neither work in the colony nor give a dowry. But my father said that he didn't want a dowry, he just wanted her as a bride. My father was already in love with her and did not want to leave. When my mother said to him that she could not work in the fields, my father replied that she would be like a princess with him...

The engagement contract was written, gifts were bought, and later the wedding was celebrated...my mother told me everything...

6.

After the wedding, the big problems started immediately. My grandpa had a really big house, but it was a very big family as well. My father's oldest brother, *Motl Shmuel*, had a wife with two children already, and they were also living together with my grandfather and with their family. So you can imagine how cramped it was there...

Attached to the house was a little hut ["shtibl"], and my father and mother had to live there. The little room was in back of the brick house and had a small window. The stove there had no chimney and there was no foundation, the floor was made of earth and was wetted as if by a river; when it was wet outside, the water was up to the knees. There was no toilet, and one had to do one's natural needs outside under the window. The pigs used to come by and eat the excrement. In winter, when snow fell and the pigs did not come, one usually stepped in the dirt. You can imagine what kind of life that was...

My mother actually could not work in the fields, but she could sew very beautiful men's shirts, which were called "oyber-hemder". There were no sewing machines at that time, and so you had to sew by hand. Aristocratic courts were located near the colony, and from there she was usually given work assignments. She was a very good seamstress and had a lot of work. However, this earned her a lot of enmity in the house. The stepmother and the sister-in-law incited my father against my mother. Thus began quarrels and life became bitter for both of them...

(Page 13)

Now I will tell you why it was so difficult for my mother, who was after all a girl from the city, to help my father with his work, just as the other women in the colony helped [their husbands]... One had to raise cattle, that is, cows, oxen and horses. This meant work from the very beginning. When a little calf is born, you have to take it inside for a week until it can suckle. To do this, you have to put the calf under the udder of the cow and hold it by the sides. If sometimes the cow is young and wild, so you get a kick with your foot, and you're done for now...The calf has to suckle for about two weeks, then it can be sold or slaughtered for yourself. But if you want to raise it to a cow, you have to let it suckle for three or four weeks to make it strong. You have to keep the baby calf inside so it doesn't get cold. The barn was half a block away. The cow had to be brought indoors overnight to prevent her from getting cold while calving. But my parents had no more than one alcove [1] in the hut... And in this room my parents' children were born. The eldest was me, *Rachel-Hene*, the second was my brother, *Yehoshue* [2] *-Velvel*...

When I was four and my brother two years old, my father was incited against my mother in my grandfather's house, and the result was a big quarrel between them that almost led to beatings. My mother jumped out of the window and fled to Grodno. My father chased after her with horse and cart, but did not reach her. In Grodno my mother stayed with her friends and they arranged for a reconciliation. It did not take long, however, for another fierce quarrel to break out. My mother fled again, this time to Amdur, twelve miles from the colony. Still outside this shtetl was a large yard, what we call a "farm" in America. There my mother ran in to the owner of the farm and told him the whole story of how her husband was so influenced by his father's family that he argued with her, his wife, and it was about to degenerate into acts of violence. The "posesor", that is, the farmer, hid my mom in his second room. When my father went to look for her, the farmer said that his wife was not coming home. Father began to plead, since he had two children at home, who were now abandoned.

---

[1] alkir or alker: room, closet, alcove

[2] Later we learn that the family called him "Ishye".

(Page 14)

He therefore did not want to leave without his wife. Thereupon the farmer said to him, "Young man, if you want your wife to accompany you home, you must give us your promise by handshake that you will never quarrel with her again and that you will not follow your family, who will set you against her." My father shook hands with them and promised.

7.

From then on they lived well together, but still there was no lack of sorrow and worries. Two more children were born, boys. One died when he was one and a half years old; his name was *Abraham Berl*, after my mother's father. The second boy, *Mendl*, lived only a week and a half after his circumcision, and my mother lamented and cried day and night. After the two children who died, she had another boy. He was given the name *Yakev-Moyshe* and was a tender child. Therefore, he was given an additional name, *Alter* [1]. This served as a defense against the evil eye. After that, my mother gave birth to another son who was named *Note* after her uncle, her father's brother. Later, a girl was born who was named *Sheyne Gitl*. She was really a beauty. She was named *Gitl* after my father's sister, and *Sheyne* after my mother's grandmother. After that a boy was born whose name was *Simkhe-Berl*, I don't remember who he was named after.

After all this, life became really difficult. We could no longer live in the little hut, we had to see how to get a bigger dwelling. My father sold an ox and a cow and looked for a house to buy. Not far away was a village, Minketse, where a gentile wanted to sell his old cottage after he had built a new one for himself. This old cottage was bought by my father. But how was the cottage brought over to the colony? It was a very difficult undertaking. There was no company that transported a house from one place to another, as in America. So how did they manage it anyway? In the colony there were large wagons. They removed the side walls from them and

---

[1] Alter "old one" is one of the amuletic names, often given to a newborn child in order to confuse the Angel of Death, in the hope that he would go looking for somebody younger or somebody else.

(Page 15)

unhitched the oxen. Then they attached one wagon to the other, dug out the cottage and put it on two wagons. A couple of horses were harnessed and the cottage was brought to us in the colony...it had to be pulled across fields and meadows.

<h2 style="text-align:center">8.</h2>

In the little house there was a large room with a chamber. Actually, the house was not very suitable, because it was too small, but one thanked God for finally living alone and not having to quarrel with Grandpa's family anymore. A stable was added for the cattle, not a big stable, because there was no room for that at all. The stable was like a kind of antechamber. It boiled down to the fact that we lived together with the cattle. If you wanted to get into our living area, you had to go through the antechamber, which was always wet from the cattle.

In the parlor, there was a small stove, consisting of a high wall, which, in the middle, was drawn a little wide at the top [1]. This was called "lezhanke" [fireplace couch]. In winter, the "lezhanke" was heated to make it warm. People sat on the "lezhanke" and warmed themselves... I remember sitting on the "lezhanke" with my little brothers and warming myself.

There was a baking oven where we baked bread for the whole week and challah for Shabbat. In summer, the small oven was not heated, however, in the baking oven we cooked a whole week, not inside the oven, but only in the front, on the so-called "pripetshik". The stove already had a chimney, not like in the previous apartment. Usually, on the big stove slept the children. There were many windows in the cottage. The roof was made of straw. There was no foundation of boards, which is called "floor" in America. The floor was made of earth. When it was very wet in the room in winter, one used to pour yellow sand on the floor.

In winter, the house was heated with peat, which was very smelly. However, usually the windows were not opened. In winter one used to smear the windows with glue and put a double window inside.

---

[1] see https://snowymelodie.livejournal.com/17668.html

Ashes were poured between the windows and colorful pieces of paper were poured on the ashes. Usually,

(Page 16)

the windows were also glued with paper so that no little [cold] air could get in. Well, in the parlor it got damp and your head used to hurt because there was not a bit of air in the house, but there was a remedy. You cut raw potatoes, put them on your head, tied a bandana around it and went to sleep...

I wrote before that in our house there was a big room with a chamber. The big room was called a "fale," which means "front room" in America. The chamber would be called a "bed-room" in America. The chamber was not large, there was a bed in it. Straw was put in the bed and sheets from white sacks were put on the straw. One used to make themselves more comfortable by making a mattress out of straw. The straw was covered with very coarse linen. When the linen was torn, the straw would fall under the bed. When the little children wet themselves, the straw would rot. One used to dry the straw mattress outside. When Passover came, the rotten straw was removed and fresh straw was put in.

There was also a sleeping bench in the chamber. At night one used to unfold the bench and the children slept on it. There was also straw in the sleeping bench... The bed was made of wood, just like the sleeping bench, and it was not very stable. It usually broke and the boards fell out. Therefore, one used to put blocks under it, so that one did not fall out of the bed....For the whole winter yellow sand was provided, which was poured under the bed and under the sleeping bench. The "fale" was also covered with yellow sand...The bench was made of boards, and the boards were placed on blocks. If you were not careful when sitting down you tipped over with the boards. The table was also made of boards...There were no chairs, only those little benches with two feet on one side, and two feet on the other. That was the furniture of the poor colonists.

To store laundry and other things, one had a chest. Valuable things were not owned. The other clothes and cloths were hung on the stove, where the children slept...

At Passover one used to clean and scrub the house, water the dishes[1] and make everything kosher. The table and benches

(Page 17)

were also scoured and made kosher, because after all, leaven had been placed on them. On the evening before Passover, all leaven had to be removed from the house. The leaven was sold to the rabbi and he used to sell it to a gentile...

As I grew older, I didn't like the table and benches on blocks. Not far from the colony was a small town, Adelsk [Odelsk]. There I knew a well-known carpenter. I went to him, and he made for me beautiful, long benches from one wall to the other, and a square table with a drawer in the middle. My mother sewed muslin curtains with wide crocheted hems[2], and the house was already decorated and very nicely dressed up...

---

[1] Glassware was soaked for three days, other cookware (pots, cutlery) was boiled to make it kosher.

[2] literally "with groyse zembes", I assume this means large crocheted air stitches that look like teeth, but I don't know for sure.

9.

When I was ten or twelve years old, we no longer had enough to live on. My father owned very little land, only one-third of a numbered field, and you couldn't live on that. One had to raise calves and, if possible, raise them into cows. Once they became cows, it was easier, but it took two years to milk the cows. You needed three or four cows to milk, otherwise you just didn't have enough for the family to live on. When you had cows and milked them, you usually made butter and cheese from the milk, so during the summer you would take the butter and cheese to Sokółka every two weeks to sell. I was about twelve years old then, and Sokółka was 18 miles from the colony. Sometimes, when there was no cart, I, a young girl, had to go on foot...

When we had a horse and cart, I used to drive to Sokółka myself with the dairy products, taking with me a few other women who also had dairy products to sell. Each of them paid 25 kopecks for the ride there and back...

[Even when we] had a horse and cart, father [often] needed the horse for farming. We raised horses and oxen. If you didn't have anything to give the cattle to eat, you had to

(Page 18)

sell the horse or the ox in autumn. When it became summer and there was no horse or ox, gentiles had to be hired for farming, and my father had to go to the city to earn money. He went to Bialystok and worked as a bricklayer, carrying heavy drawers of stones or bricks. We were already a big family, and three boys who had to go to the kheyder [Jewish religious elementary school].

At harvest time, Father used to come home from Bialystok to cut the fields, because otherwise gentiles would have had to be hired. Early on, the barley was cut, because if you did not cut it in time, the ears poured out. Then we began to cut the rye and then the wheat, then the oats, the peas and also the lentils. Buckwheat did not need to be cut, but only torn off.

When everything was harvested, people began to pick up the potatoes. Potatoes had to be planted in the field and later dug out of the ground. This was hard work. For a whole day one had to lie on the ground and dig the potatoes out of the wet earth. It was then already cold and rain fell more often. However, you had to take out the potatoes, you could not leave them in the field about overnight, so you had to be in the field until late at night.

Then, when you got home late, the first thing you had to do was milk the cows, and after that cook dinner for the family...

10.

I have to tell you beforehand about the difficulties during the grain harvest. Our field was divided into several places. One part of the field was far away, about three vyorst [3,1 km], but you had to be in the field early in the morning around seven, sometimes even earlier, to cut the grain. I still remember how Mom had the little child in her arms, carrying it the whole three vyorst. In addition, you had to take a jug of water to drink for the whole day, also bread, butter, cheese, hard-boiled eggs, and for the toddler something to drink. Actually, it should have sucked,

(Page 19)

but since Mom worked hard, there was nothing for the toddler to suck...

It would not have been good to simply lay the infant down in the field, so it was necessary to quickly cut a few bundles of grain and set them up like a small hut so that the sun would not burn the child and the wind would not, God forbid, chill him. What could one do but trust in God's help when it began to rain, thunder and lightning. One erected "vodonoskes" from the bundles of grain. These were twelve bundles, nine were placed on the side and three were placed on top so that it would not rain through to the bottom. One could not go home, certainly not with a small child. The field bordered the village of Krasleski, and if the rain didn't stop, you had to walk barefoot all the way there...

In summer, people went barefoot; who could afford to walk in shoes? If you had old slippers, you would walk in them. Before the harvest we used to mow the meadows to have hay for the animals for the winter. The cut hay had to be turned with a rake so that it would dry. At night the hay had to be piled up in a mountain, so that in case of rain it would not get wet, only the top part. When you had piled the hay into a mountain and it rained, you could hide inside the hay.

Life was very hard for a small colonist, like my father. Those who had many fields could afford to hire gentiles. In fact, in winter we still had to buy bran for the cattle so that they did not emaciate. Since my father ground the rye in the mill, he usually had litter left over from the grain. The litter was made into "shetshke", chopped straw mixed with rye flour, and given to the cattle to eat...But if you gave the grain to the cattle, you didn't have enough to eat even in the summer. One had to go and borrow something. Since one was not allowed to borrow from Jews, one went to the gentiles in Odelsk.

If one did not have enough flour to bake bread, one took peas, potatoes or lentils instead of bread. And sometimes one deceived the children, then one mixed potatoes into the rye flour. It was not as good as

(Page 20)

pure rye flour...If you had beet, you cooked "borshtsh", beet soup. If there was again no meat for the whole week, one bought a herring, and so one was already good friends with the grocer. The grocer gave you some "lyok", herring sauce, when you bought a herring from him. You boiled the potatoes in their skins and dipped them in "lyok", or you doused the potatoes with "lyok".

In the fall one slaughtered a few sheep or a calf, salted the meat, and this was enough for the Shabbats of the whole winter, sometimes even for Passover...One raised geese in the winter, so that one had a little "shmalts" [fat] for Passover...The meat and the fat were kept in the cellar. One dug a special pit in the cellar, put the meat and fat in a particular vessel, which we called "kodke", put stones on it, and it remained fresh until Passover...

11.

I forgot to tell you that in the summer we ourselves led the cattle to pasture. There were indeed drovers, but they herded everyone's animals and there was not enough grass for all the animals [in their pastures]. Therefore, we ourselves drove the animals to other places where there was enough grass to graze. We got up at three o'clock in the morning and drove the animals to the pastures, and at eight o'clock we brought them back for milking. If they had grazed well, they gave a lot of milk...One then slept for a few hours and afterwards drove the cattle again on the pasture, all this was done during the day. In the evening, the cattle were brought home and milked again... The milk was poured into "ladishtshikes", clay jugs, wrapped in linen cloth and placed in the cellar to produce sour cream and sour milk. From the sour cream one made butter, and from the sour milk one made cheese. When butter was churned [from the milk cream], a residual liquid remained, which we called "mashlintse" [buttermilk]. We drank this and also made cheese from it, which we called "mashlinke" [sic] cheese. We did not sell this cheese, but consumed it ourselves.

(Page 21)

If we did not drive the cows to pasture ourselves, but handed them over to the shepherd, we had to go and get grass, because the cattle came home hungry in the evening. But that was much harder work. We walked across the furrows and boundaries to pluck the grass and were afraid that the owner of the field would come and beat us up. Dragging the grass was also very difficult, we were completely tangled in it.

After we cut the grain, we drove the cattle to the harvested field, and the animals still found enough to graze there...I have already told you that the chopped straw, which we called "shetshke", was mixed with the rye flour or bran and given to the cattle to eat in the winter...We had a lot of potato peelings and mixed them with the "shetshke" as well. When there was a big frost, we boiled the potato peels in water and gave this to the animals to warm them up...In winter we also used to spread straw on the earth in the stable so that the animals would not be too cold when they lay down...

We also raised poultry. For Passover we had the chickens incubate the eggs; we had then young poultry for Rosheshone [Rosh HaShanah] and chickens for Yom Kippur "far kapores" [for the ceremony of the atonement]. Thus, we also had eggs for the children to eat. In winter we had very few eggs, because the chickens laid only a few, so we had to purchase some...At Passover we processed many eggs, because we prepared "halkes" [dumplings] and also "pampushkes"[fritters], and so we needed many eggs...

From the fat we prepared for Passover, we usually sold some too, and that helped us to buy shirts for the children for Passover...All winter long the children went in coarse linen shirts, and for Passover they bought a bit of thin linen fabric to sew nice shirts for the holiday. As you already know, my Mom was a good seamstress...I still remember how the neighbors came to my mother and asked her to cut quite a few shirts for their children...but my mother usually did not just cut them or give instructions on how to sew them. My mother considered [sewing them together] a "mitsve" [religious commandment, good deed]...

I'll tell you now how they used to dress up the little boys: they sewed for them little pants and vests made of "kort" [corduroy].

(Page 22)

A short jacket was called a "munarke", and a vest was called a "kamuzoylke", both were sewn for Passover... for Sukkoth warm things were sewn. Instead of a "munarke" one sewed a "kapotke", an overcoat, and this was lined with absorbent cotton to keep the children warm. The "kamuzoylke" was also padded so that the children did not get cold. The "munarke" was short, while the "kapotke" was long, so that the children did not freeze on their legs...

If you had a little more money, you could afford to let a tailor sew the clothes for the boys...Boots were made by a cobbler, they could not be bought anywhere else...Also for the girls you sewed yourself, a dress or a "spodnitse" [skirt][1] and a blouse. Sewing a dress or an underdress was not as difficult as sewing for the boys. I sewed myself things, skirts, blouses and sometimes a dress...In the winter you had to wear a "vatofke", which was something similar to an undergarment. With us [in America] they call it a "pedekout" [petticoat].

In Odelsk there was a dressmaker, and if you could afford it, you bought a piece of woolen cloth and gave it to the [female] dressmaker. When the girls grew up, they already wore nicer clothes. On Shabbat and holidays they dressed up. There were already tailors in the small towns of Sokółka, Krynki or Amdur, and people usually went there to buy some dresses or a coat for the holiday or for a wedding...in these towns there were ladies tailors...

When the girls got older, they had to go to the big cities to work. There, the girls were already following the fashion...

I forgot to write what the boys had to wear when they went to the kheyder [cheder] in winter. In the winter there were hard frosts and a lot of snow; you walked in the snow up to your knees. There were no overshoes, so the boys had to wear boots and warm woolen socks. One knitted the socks oneself from coarse wool. There was also need for a fur coat, so one bought a few sheepskins from the "goyim" [gentiles] to sew a sheepskin coat so that the children would not get cold. If you didn't have a fur coat, you bought coarse cloth fabric and lined it with velvet to make it warmer...

(Page 23)

12.

In the colony, boys had to go to cheder, whether you could afford it or not. It was not only in our colony, but all over Europe...a boy had to be able to pray and also learn a little "khumesh" [Pentateuch] with [commentaries of] Rashi and read "sedre" [the portions of the Torah]. But these were really only basics of the subject matter. The boys who later also wanted to study "gemore" [part of the Talmud] and "mishnayes" [six mishna portions, the oldest texts of the Talmud] grew up to be "lamdonim", Jewish scholars. When there was nothing to eat, the parents hired or borrowed something, but the children had to be sent to the cheder...The poor parents, who had no means to buy a fur coat or a piece of cloth to sew warm clothes for their boys, sent them off in tattered boots and torn jackets, which were already hanging in shreds; but even from the shirts, shreds were already hanging down...

The boys attended the cheder from eight o'clock in the morning until eight o'clock in the evening...If there was frost or snow, they were given their midday meal to take to school...some poor mothers, unfortunately, even had to send their children off hungry, because when there was nothing to eat, they still had to go to the cheder...

---

[1] a "spodnitse" is usually a petticoat or underdress, but I think that Rachel means a "skirt"

Now I want to describe to you the cheder, that is, the "shtibl", [the classroom in the house] of the Rebbe. The "shtibl" consisted of a room and a chamber. In winter it was wet and cold. The windows were covered with paper on both sides, so that the boys didn't have a bit of fresh air all day long. They used to feed the Rebbe's children one more time, and the Rebbe used to spank them violently...But it was better for the boys if the teacher was stricter, because if they were afraid of the teacher, they learned better. Some boys got sick from the wetness and humidity in the Rebbe's room...I haven't written the slightest bit about how the boys suffered there, but at least they grew up to be good Jews...

The girls were not taught in those years, they were not sent to the cheder...In the small towns the parents did not mind that the girls could not learn. They were only occupied with the boys, so that they could learn Hebrew, read the Pentateuch and the Torah portions...When the boys got older, around 10 or 12 years old, they were sent

(Page 24)

to the big cities, to the "talme-toyres" [the free community schools for the poor] and to the "yeshives" [Talmud schools]... For them, the "esn teg" [daily meal] was established, that is, certain richer citizens undertook in turn to give the "yeshive-bokher" [student at the yeshive] food in their house for [at least] one day. If the boys were not offered enough days to eat, they had to starve.

Richer parents sent money to their boys so that they did not have to go hungry. Unfortunately, however, the poor went hungry when they could not find a house to eat in for one or two days a week...But considering that they grew up and were able to study well, they were lucky, because they later received a large dowry and quite a few years of "kest" [good food]...

Some hired a private teacher for their boys. In this way, also the girls could learn a little Yiddish from him, to write and to pray. But this only happened with wealthy parents: Among the poor people and also among the colonists it was very rare that the girls could learn to write and pray.

13.

In the shtetl Odelsk the girls usually plucked feathers in winter and got ten kopecks for a pound. Those girls who were nimble could earn a ruble a week. They also did other work, knitting woolen stockings, gloves and also socks. If you didn't wear woolen socks, stockings and gloves, your feet and hands would freeze...In our colony the girls also plucked feathers and made woolen stockings, socks and gloves. They worked for the "goyim" and earned between twenty and thirty rubles. From this money they equipped themselves with clothes for Passover...Before Passover, the girls also went to the larger towns, unrolling matzos. This also helped them financially to dress for Passover and throughout the summer... In the summer the girls went to cut grain, either at the "goyim" in Odelsk or at our colony, and for this they dressed for Rosh Hashanah, Yom Kippur and Sukkoth... And when one had dressed, young boys from Krynki, Amdur or Sokółka used to come on the semi-holidays

(Page 25)

of Passover or Sukkot. One became acquainted with each other and soon one became a bride... Some girls who were not too proud to do so went to the surrounding towns as maids, but some were also ashamed to do so and continued to toil away with their poor parents...

When I was a child of 10 or 12, I worked with my father at a place in Bialystok where they baked matzos for Passover. My father was a deliverer of the matzos and I was a "velgerin", that is, I rolled out the matzos. When I was ten years old, my father was already the head of the family of one wife and four children. My father did not own a large field, only a third of a field number, and so he could not make a living from it. But one had to clothe the children at Passover and pay tuition to the Rebbe. Therefore, my father went to Bialystok or Grodno already a few months before Passover, to order in advance a place in a bakery as a delivery boy of matzos...The baker who baked the matzos that the "balebatim", the heads and owners of households, ordered from him for Passover, needed one employee to bake the matzos, one to "redlen" the matzos [to perforate with an intended wheel] and one to deliver the matzos to the houses. My father had to order his job as a matzos deliverer three months before Passover, because if you waited the last few weeks before Passover, the job was already taken.

The owner of the bakery, which was called "pekarnye", did not pay the deliverer, nor the "redler", nor the baker, nor the kneader or the roller of the dough. The "householders" who ordered the matzos at the bakery gave each of the workers a few rubles. The worker who stood by the oven and watched that the matzos did not burn got more than [most of the others]...In contrast, the "redler" did not get so much. But the deliverer received even more than the man who stood by the oven. The kneader got more than the dough roller. There was also a "water pourer", who was always a little boy or girl. Also the "water-pourers" did not receive their from the owner of the bakery, but from the "balebatim" who had ordered the matzos. If the "balebatim" were wealthy, the workers received more; from the poorer "balebatim" they understandably

(Page 26)

received less...a large family baked[1] more matzos than a smaller one...

In addition to matzos, one had to provide wine, meat and fat for Passover and clothe the children...My father had to pay for the festive customs for Passover from his income as a deliverer of matzos, he also had to pay the debts of the previous winter that he had incurred from others. If my father obtained a position in a good bakery where many wealthy "balebatim" ordered their matzos, my father could not only provide for a proper Passover in the house, but also pay off all the debts...

When I was a girl of 12, I asked my father to take me to Bialystok to roll out ("velgern") the matzos. I would like to be able to dress for Passover and put on a nice dress and nice shoes, just like other girls...But it was not so easy as I tell you here. No, you had to stand on your feet in in the bakery from seven in the morning until eight at night...

_____

[1] I think she means "ordered"

My father did not have enough money to rent a room for me in Bialystok, so we went to my mom's cousin, a water carrier, who carried buckets of water on a water pole to poor heads of households, and therefore he barely earned a living. When my father took me to see the water carrier in the apartment, I became gloomy. It was only one room, completely full, plus a toddler. The woman was not beautiful, with warts on her face and "splattered wet like a duck". Her husband was short and hunched over from carrying the heavy buckets of water. But however poor he was, he was good to me, and so was his wife. Like the pure angels. I stayed with them for three weeks. When I came home at night, I had to eat for dinner what the water carrier's wife had left for me. I had not seen such dear people before, poor and simple, but so good. What a pity I have forgotten their names, but so much time has passed since then, about 73 years. May their souls rest in Gan Eden [the Garden of Eden]...

14.

I remember how my father took my little brother Yehoshue Velvel, wrapped him in a "tales" [prayer shawl], carried him first to the Bes-Hamedresh

(Page 27)

and later to the cheder so that he would grow up to be a good Jew and learn. In fact, he did learn well, but he did not become a pious Jew. My brother Yehoshue will soon be 83 years old and before he was born, two of my parent's children died. Since Yehoshue Velvel was such a tender child, he was carried in the "tales" into the Bes-Hamedresh, this was to serve as an amulet...However, as I said, now he will soon be 83 years old and has three married sons and a daughter...

I am two and a half years older than Yehoshue Velvel. After him, two more children were born and I had to feed the children because my mother was busy milking the cows and taking the cattle to pasture. At that time I was not even five years old. As I have written before, there was neither a toilet nor a bathroom in our home. The children were bathed in a tub, from which the cows also ate...You had to carry the water from the well, and there were no faucets or sinks, like in America, where you just have to do a twist to make the cold or hot water run. You had to carry two buckets of water from the well on a "karomisle" [water carrier pole], and the well was three blocks from home...In the summer, sometimes the water in the well would dry up...

In the tub, where the children were bathed, the adults also washed on Shabbat. It was a wooden tub, in which one washed also laundry. For this purpose, a few buckets of water were heated. One shook out the laundry and then toiled oneself with it on a board...

For Rosheshone [Rosh HaShanah] one went to the bath. The bath was a vyorst [1,06 km] away from our colony, and if one wanted to indulge oneself, one also went there on Passover, but only the men. The children were taken to the bath only on Rosh HaShanah and Yom-Kiper [Yom Kippur]...

Not far from us there was a small river and I remember how we girls used to wash out the clothes and wash cloths on a board there in the summer, but it was not a washboard, just a simple board.

The women of the colony went to the baths when they had to go to the mikveh and once they had to go every

(Page 28)

month, and even when there was frost and snow. I still remember how my mother used to take me with her. The women paid the "beder" [supervisor in the bath] 25 kopeks, then he heated the water...

The "beder" was always poorly off. He might have been the most beautiful person, but he was not considered a respectable person. The girls did not want to make friends with the daughters of the bath attendant, don't ask me why...

In severe frost and snowfall, when the road was covered with snow, the women went to the mikveh in the well...This is what my mother herself told me. We had heavy frosts and whole mountains of snow. It could have cost one's life to go to Odelsk for a bath. Therefore, the men chopped an opening in the [frozen] river, and the women immersed themselves either there or in the well...

Sometimes you scooped out all the water for the animals or the water was frozen, then you had to go to the mikveh in the river. My mother also went either to the river or to the well. My father prepared the mikveh, which was used in winter, during heavy frost and snowstorms. In summer, on the other hand, it was more bearable...

I forgot to write that the well was very deep and one had to let the woman down with a rope. In case the well was not so deep, a ladder was used to go down...The women were not allowed to postpone going to the mikveh for a single day, because it was considered the greatest sin, for which one might go to hell...

After the mikveh, the "beder" had to stand at the door and the women had to look at him. The "beder" had to be a pious Jew. If he was not pious, one was not allowed to look at him. If one's own husband was already approaching, one directed one's gaze at him...

There was a great fear that, God forbid, one would be attacked after leaving the mikveh, because the bath was not far from the homes of the "goyim". Therefore, the women would ask the "beder" if he knew which of the neighbors would have to go to the mikveh in the evening to have an escort. The husbands also went out to meet [the women], so that their fear decreased. The men were not allowed to know that the neighbor's

(Page 29)

wife had also gone to the mikveh; but if one met [by chance] next to the bath, it was not considered a sin. It was considered a blessing for a woman to look at a pious Jew after the mikveh, because then her children, whom she later bore, would become pious Jews.

15.

Now I will tell you about the time when I was a child of eight to ten. As I wrote before, I fed the children [siblings]. In the winter, it was not often possible to bathe the children; the small children were washed only once a week, on the Friday before Shabbat. When I remember those times, a shudder runs through me. Head lice poured from the heads when I washed the children and combed their hair. But there were also [dandruff and] other particles ["materye"] falling from their heads, which were almost completely scabbed over. They had incipient scab, and their sores were such that they could not be washed or combed. The lice were also already in the shirts and all over the body there were bites...On Shabbat one had the time to delouse the children; and also the adults deloused themselves...

There was a lot of pity for the children. Their hair hung matted and tangled. This was not only the case with our children, but [the hair of] all the children in the entire colony was lice-ridden and tangled. They smeared their heads with gray ointment, tied a rag around them overnight and tore it off early in the morning. The screams reached up to the sky...So you went to the cheder with pain. But no one needed to be ashamed, because after all, in the winter all the children had rash on their heads, and all the children had frazzled hair, no one was a distinguished aristocrat...It was said that this was because so much sand was used in the house. One had sand to lie under the beds, a lot of it also under the benches; everywhere in the house was sand. One made a stock of sand for the whole winter, because when there was snow in the winter, one didn't get any sand. But I remember when I was a little girl and the snow had thawed a bit, I used to gather sand with another girl. You couldn't get along without sand because it was just very wet in the house...

(Page 30)

I forgot to mention that there was no electricity either. Well, with what could one make light in the house? One usually had a kerosene lamp with a little glass that was always sooty and black with smoke, and it also stank of kerosene. Kerosene was called "gaz". And we used the "gaz" very sparingly. You know what we did? We bought pine wood, dried it, cut it and chopped it into small logs. We dried the logs and split them into very thin pieces, as thin as paper and as narrow as a bread knife...With this material, the "drazges", we lit the house. But you can imagine that the whole house was full of smoke from it. Only on Shabbat and when we plucked feathers at night we filled the lamp with "gaz"...

While the "drazges" were burning, we were afraid of a possible fire. If a fire had broken out, it would have meant great misfortune, because the houses were not insured...In winter we plucked many feathers, and when we were done with it, we knitted stockings and socks, gloves and who could, also vests, and everything at the sooty little lamp...

What I am writing here was 77 years ago. At that time I was eight or nine years old and could make beautiful tablecloths and blankets for the beds. I could sew little birds, ducks and flowers and hang them on the wall...one thought I was very talented. I don't want to boast about it, but this is what they said about me...Even as a child I helped around the house. When I was only six years old, I was already helping to raise the children.

16.

Still in the colony, at the age of eight, I learned to roll out matzos...Every head of household had to have matzos for Passover after all, and so ten to twelve neighbors got together and baked the matzos at the house of whoever had the biggest oven...My parents, who also needed matzos for Passover, also got together with others, and I helped

(Page 31)

unroll ("velgern") the matzos...I forgot to tell you that the man who pushed the matzos into the oven on a shovel was called a "zetser," that is, he "put" the matzos into the oven.

One had to be good at kneading the matzos. If a kneader could not knead well and left a few crumbs, the entire matzos dough was considered soured and could not be used...I watched the kneader knead and soon learned to do so, so I could help the kneader and she was very grateful to me...

In our colony there was also a bakery where matzos was baked for everyone for a fee, and all the wealthy heads of households in the colony and surrounding villages had matzos baked in this bakery...The wife of the bakery's owner paid one ruble a day. I earned eight to ten rubles at Passover, and made myself some clothes and a coat from the money. It was a great joy to be able to get clothes for yourself...

The people who ran the bakery were old. The man's name was *Dovid Leyzer* and she was called *Peshe Leye*. He had a son by his first wife, *Avrohem Itse*, and she had a daughter by her first husband, named *Libe*. They were married off. Libe was an important boss. From her I learned to become a good "velgerin"...Avrohem Itse was small in stature. He used to plow the field with oxen. His oxen were very big...Libe and Avrohem Itse had five children – two daughters and three sons. One daughter was called *Tsirl*, and I became friends with her. We herded cattle together in the pastures. The second daughter, *Khaye Feygl*, was not a beauty. She was cross-eyed...Her older brother, *Shmuel Yankel*, celebrated his wedding in the shtetl Yaneva, not far from the colony, with the daughter of a noble, rich man. Shmuel Yankel was an eminent Jewish scholar, and therefore he received a large dowry and quite a few years of "kest" [financial support]. For such was the custom in those days: you only got a Jewish scholar for a son-in-law if you gave your daughter a large dowry and "kest" for several years...It goes without saying that poor parents who could not give a large dowry married their daughters to laborers...The second brother, *Mordekhay Moyshe*,

(Page 32)

had been ordained as a rabbi and married the daughter of a very rich man, he received a very large dowry and "kest" for 10 years...

My friend Tsirl had a wedding with one from the shtetl Sokhevola [Suchowola], not far from the colony. Her parents could give only 300 rubles for her dowry, and even this sum was difficult for her to raise, but they had to arrange a prestigious wedding because of her brothers...

There was no doctor in the colony. When a woman gave birth to a child, they called *Khaye-Peshe*, the old woman in whose house the bakery had been...She had very skillful hands, and therefore she was even called by women to Odelsk for or after childbirth...

It sometimes happened that a birth turned out to be difficult, then a doctor had to be brought from Krynki or Grodno...When my mama gave birth to a child, I ran to call Khaye-Peshe as soon as possible. She was a unique woman, a good soul...Peshe Leye was called "di bobe", "the grandmother". She, the "bobe", helped in the birth of all my sisters and brothers...When she passed away, her daughter, Libe, became "di bobe".

17.

And now I want to tell you how men were escorted to Russia as prisoners. I saw this with my own eyes, back when I was a child. There were big frosts and the snow was high up to the roof, so you couldn't go out of the house. The snowstorms could whirl people into the air. In these conditions, people were herded in convoy, and can you imagine what that meant? If a poor person was seized without a passport, they would drive him on foot from one village to another, from one town to another, hundreds of miles, all the way to his birthplace.

I remember how the little children took pity on the detainees and brought them something to eat, because they were hungry. I remember it as clearly as if it had just happened today...In Russia, if one had broken any law and was seized, the prisoner fared very badly. He was severely beaten and put in the "kartser", that is, in a dark chamber...

(Page 33)

I remember how my father's brother, *Artshik*, used to hide in our attic. This was covered with straw, and during the hard frosts Artshik slept in the straw at night. My father carried food up to him...

One night we saw the village chief with two convicts looking for him. What a fright we got! My uncle escaped through the roof...Why was he hiding? He was to be drafted as a recruit! Though he had drawn the highest number, he still was afraid that his number would come up. Therefore he hid himself. But it turned out that the necessary number of recruits had already been collected, so that his number did not come up at all. So he did not have to go to the military service.

18.

Now I will write about my life when I was about 13 or 14, until I turned 18. I remember that my father went to work in a dyeworks factory in Bialystok. The income from cultivating his field was not enough to support himself. There were other people from the colony working in the factory who could not live on agriculture alone either. One from the colony lived in the house right next to us. His name was *Yehoshua Etke's*. His mother was called Etke. People called each other by their first name or added their mother's or father's name. The aforementioned Yehoshue Eke's had gone to Bialystok before my father to work in the factory and immediately requested a job there for my father.

And do you know what they earned in a week? Three and a half rubles. For that they worked from 6 o'clock in the morning to 6 o'clock in the evening...My father's older brother also worked in the same factory. The factory owner was called Arke Saraske [alias *Aharon* or *H. Suraski*], he was the biggest factory owner in Bialystok. The factory was a few vyorst from Bialystok, and the factory yard was huge, miles in length and in width. There was steam-powered machinery and hundreds of people working there.

My father had taken me there to be apprenticed. He rented a place for me to stay in the yard of the factory

(Page 34)

with a poor weaver, for 14 kopecks a week. The weaver's wife wound "kete" ["warp"] and she taught me to wind the warp onto the large bobbins. As soon as I had learned to spool, I got a job. But I found it very difficult to turn the spinning wheel with the wool, and constantly the skeins of wool tangled up...The wool had "konitses" [ending bits], and because everything got tangled with me, I tore out whole pieces and inserted them between the end pieces. But when they checked the ending bits, they saw that I had added too much wool there...I was fired! When I worked next to my father in the same factory building, my father and other workers from the factory used to cook food for themselves. My father cooked a little more, so I could go and see him and eat a little too, at least if there was anything left.

I have already told you that my father and the other workers earned three and a half rubles a week. But they had to save some of that and send it home to their wives and children. They usually went to town on Sunday and bought coarse-grained bread, barley for "krupnik" [barley soup], a few herrings with lyok [herring sauce] and potatoes. It was already considered a luxury if you had herring in addition to the potatoes that you dipped in lyok... On Shabbat they bought meat and other good things, and this was really "keyad hamelekh" [as befits a king]...

When I worked near my dad in the same factory complex, he paid for me to dine at the weaver's wife on Shabbat. However, when I lost my job, I was in a very bad way. I was not yet 15 years old at that time. I looked for work in the factories near father, but I could not work there. It was because they were "goyish" [gentile] factories, where people worked until late at night, and it was dangerous to go home at night. So I went to look for work in the city, but it was extremely difficult before I could then earn anything...

19.

Now I will describe to you the factory owner *Arke Saraske*, who paid the workers three and a half rubles. He was a prominent Hasid and used to go to the Volozher [Volozhiner] Rabbi. He did not look after

(Page 35)

women, but if he caught a young girl who was alone, one had great difficulty in escaping from his hands. Likewise, the whole family, his sons and sons-in-law, were hypocritical Hasids, and all were rich scoundrels...

The girls had already agreed among themselves that it was better not to go alone to the factory store... And such millionaires paid a head of a family three and a half rubles a week...A few years later, however, people wised up and started to strike, so the factory owners ("balebatim") got into trouble, but they still had it better than the workers...

Now let's go back to the time when I was laid off from my job...My father went to the city to find a place for me to stay. For a room I had to pay one ruble a month, but how could I pay one ruble, I was not earning anything. My father was told about an apartment where a woman lived with her husband and their little girl... The husband was a big fool, a real "idiot", and the little girl was also mentally handicapped, just like her father. In fact, the man was the son of a rich man, but the woman had poor parents. One concealed the truth from the idiot and the young woman. The rich father promised all the happiness in the world if only the poor young woman would marry his son, the idiot. The rich father had a farm with houses. In the back of the yard, where the neighbors washed their clothes, there was a small apartment...In there the woman lived with her husband and the girl. It was only one room, without an "optrit", that is, as we say in America, a toilet. There was only a high fence from which you could open a board, making use of this as an "optrit".

In this room the poor woman had two more girls staying, one of them was me. We both slept in one bed, and that was such a bed! It was just lined with a bit of shredded straw... Oy, that was a life as bitter as radish...I toiled for a long time and found no work. I learned to work as a "shererke" [warper][1]. But to be a "shererke" you needed a "pul" [pull, here: recommendation], as they say in America. Since I didn't get a job as a "shererke", I used to work a bit as a warp spooler. This pleased me and I learned to "nupn"[2] the pieces of fabric

(Page 36)

that the weaver had finished. One had to carefully pick out the "nodules" so that no small holes formed. This made a lot of work, but brought little reward...

Arriving home from work, you had to eat something. The "baleboste", the lady of the house, was a good one and had already prepared some supper. I paid a total of 50 kopecks a week. What kind of supper that was, oh my..., but at least it kept one alive. The woman also prepared some food for me on Shabbat...

I forgot to tell you that our bed was a sleeping bench where the child lay during the day, so it was wet, but, [as they said], "If you can't go over the top, you have to go underneath"...

My younger brother, Yehoshue Velvel, studied on the same street in the Bes-Hamedresh and came to eat with me on Shabbat. Then I thanked God that this shabby flophouse had at least such a good "baleboste"...

Behind the small apartment was a laundry. There I usually washed my and my brother's clothes on Sunday, and that led me to continue living in such a poor place...When I got tired of it, I went home to our colony, spent a little time there and then returned to Bialystok...At harvest time, I always went home to help with the grain cutting, this was more useful than loitering without work...

----

[1] The Yiddish occupational title "shererke", in German "Schärerin", in English "warper", is a technical term from weaving. "Warping" is the process of preparing warp yarn tapes for the subsequent weaving process, see: https://de.wikipedia.org/wiki/Sch%C3%A4ren

[2] The Yiddish verb "nupn" is a technical term from the weaving trade. It refers to an activity of correcting small processing defects in the finished woven fabric, for example, taking out the knots. A woman who practiced this profession was called "nuperke".

20.

All the time I was struggling to find some work in Bialystok, I lived with the woman and her moronic husband. If I could not pay, she believed my plight. And even when she already had three children of her own, I and another girl still lived with her. When I returned home and came back, I always found "my apartment" empty ... not all girls wanted to live in such a dark place...

I saw my father only once a week, on Shabbat, because his factory

(Page 37)

was too far away...He usually came to town with other workers, our colony neighbors who worked with him in the dyeworks factory...They gathered in a place we call a "restaurant" in America, but here we called it a "gorkikh" [cook shop]...It was a small place, and the "baleboste" was an old woman, but a very good one. Everyone met there. I also met there with my father. The "baleboste" from the "gorkikh" was called Leye, and she was almost deaf, unfortunately she heard almost nothing. One had to shout at her.

With Leye in the "gorkikh" served a girl from our colony. She was the daughter of Yehoshue Etke's, who worked with my father in the dyeworks factory...and I would like to add that everyone, whether it was my father, Yehoshue Etke's, or other workers, slept in the factory, embedded in woolen cloth, and covered themselves with their coats or with old quilts that one had brought from the colony.

As for Yehoshue Etke's, who lived in the house next but one from us in the colony, I still remember how they had to get a doctor from Krynki, two miles from our colony, when his wife[1] was in labor...I remember how everyone from the colony came running together to see him. But the doctor from Krynki, a very eminent doctor, could not help Yehoshue Etke's wife. By the time he arrived, it was too late...I still remember what happened after that...for a long time people could not forget the sad event, not only Yehoshue Etke's family, but everyone in our colony...There remained six orphans hanging around...After quite a few months Yehoshue Etke's held wedding with his cousin, an older poor girl...[Yehoshue's daughter], *Khaye Tamara*, a girl of 14 years, did not get along well with her stepmother. Therefore, her father took her to

Bialystok and gave her to serve in Leye's "gorkikh". Since she was so miserable, I visited her from time to time...Leye of the "gorkikh" was a good woman. When I came, she instructed Khaye Tamara to give me some food. She knew that I earned very little... Leye knew me from before, when I worked together with my father in Bialystok in the matzos bakery, where she was a co-owner...

Now and then evil swindlers came to Leye's "gorkikh". Then Leye always protected Khaya Tamara from them better than her own mother could. Her "gorkikh" was at the back of the market, next to the town clock.

---

[1] Based on the author's later statements, the wife mentioned here appears to have died later, so Yehoshue Etke's was a widower for a while, before he married again.

(Page 38)

21.

I forgot to tell you that after I lost my place in Arke Saraske's factory, a cousin of the weaver with whom I used to live, a very good young woman, taught me how to "nupn" pieces of cloth that the weaver had finished. You had to remove the "knots" without leaving holes. And if the weaver had woven in two threads instead of one, the "nuperke" had to remove it and make sure it was no longer visible. Whenever small holes had formed in other places, the "nuperke" had to plug them...But, that was still not enough for me. I wanted to do an apprenticeship as a "shererke". I liked that better; it was harder, but you could earn more...Every Shabbat the people of our colony who worked in the factory met in Leye's "gorkikh". There they ate "tsholent" [cholent], which, however, had to be credited, because, according to Jewish law, one was not allowed to pay with money on Shabbat. Once on a Shabbat I met one from the colony there, *Moyshe Kinze's*. He lived in the eighth house seen from us...and at the time his wife, *Nekhome*, had just fallen out with my mother...Nekhome's boy, *Avreml*, had been fighting with my brother, Yehushue, he threw a stone and hit my brother on the leg with it. In the process, the periosteum cracked open, and the wound began to rot and form wild flesh. You already know that there was no doctor in the colony. There was only a feldsher there who didn't recognize the nature of the injury to the leg until it had already begun to rot. My mother was very hostile to Nekhome after that...

I remember how my mother went with my brother to the eminent *doctor Prage* in Bialystok. Prage performed an operation on my brother's leg and was successful. He was able to walk again afterwards, but for many years traces remained. My brother, of whom I am writing, is now 83 years old...

(Page 39)

But now I want to come back to *Moyshe Kinze's*. Apart from the fact that my mother and his wife were very angry with each other, Moyshe was very kind to me when he met me in Leye's "gorkikh". He did me a great favor. Moyshe Kinze's was a tall, handsome man with a long beard. He was a weaver, at a time when weavers played a big role in Bialystok...I lamented to him that it was so hard for me to find a job, and if I learned to "shern ketn" [to prepare the warp yarn tapes], I might do better. I also complained to him that I didn't know who to turn to, because in order to learn the craft of warping, you would have to get a good recommendation from someone, "a pull" as they say in America. He listened to me and said that he would come back to Leye's "gorkikh" in a week for cholent and I should meet him there, maybe he would have something for me then...

In short, the next Shabbat he came with good news, namely that the "shererke" [warper] in the factory where he worked had agreed to teach me the craft of warping. It was not trained in all factories, and in this factory it was possible for the "shererke" only because her brother was the master there...She was the bride of a weaver from the same factory, his name was *Efraim Itsi Yaner's* and his father was called *Itsi Yaner's*.

Efraim Itsi Yaner's bride taught me to "shern di ketn" [to prepare the warp yarn tapes]. Previously, I had already learned to "nupn" a piece of cloth, and practiced it even in that factory on a few pieces of cloth a week. But it was very difficult to earn enough for a living, even when I had already finished my apprenticeship as a "shererke" [warper]. I had to find a factory somewhere that would hire me as a "shererke", but I didn't succeed. I was not yet known in the city, at that time I was a young girl of 15 years. Occasionally at the end of the week, I got a job to cut two warps and to "nupn" a few pieces of fabric, that were real festive days for me. This was not so much about the earnings for me, but the joy that I could already cut warps alone. A "shererke" was doing a responsible job. After all, she could have ruined a whole warp, and a warp cost a lot of money.

In time it became a "slek" [slack], as they say in America. There wasn't much work and I lost even the little bit of work I got on Thursday and Friday. What can I tell you, I got sick

(Page 40)

of moving from one factory to the next looking for work. One factory didn't need many "shererkes", there was one "shererke" for every ten weavers, and for every two weavers you needed one bobbin winder. It made me angry, and I went back to the colony. In time, however, I became estranged from the work and the factories, and when I came back to Bialystok, it was even harder for me to get work...

22.

Now my real worries began:

My father lost his job at the dyeworks factory and he came back to the colony. He bought a horse, but he couldn't buy a good one. So, he bought a cheap and lean one, because a good horse cost a lot of money. My father started to plow the small field with the horse, however, he could not give the horse good food. For that he would have had to buy oats, but he didn't have the money. [So,] the horse was fooled. It was given "shetske", that is, chopped straw with a little oats, but the horse said to it, "If you don't give me oats, then I won't go either, you'll see!" And indeed, the horse implemented his plan and refused to go. When my father went to plow the field, he had to pull not only the hook plow, but also the horse...

In Odelsk there lived a man called *Sokher*. He dealt in grain and hired my father to bring his grain to Grodno. So, when my father did not have to work in the field, he transported Sokher's grain to Grodno and on the way back brought products for the stores in Odelsk...

Sokher, a man of distinguished lineage, also ran a small store. His father, Reb Shmuel, was a great Jewish scholar who studied and taught in the Bes-Hamedresh. His wife's name was *Peshe* and she ran a bakery. I remember when I was a little girl, my mother would send me to Peshe to sell her a few pounds of butter and quite a few cheeses, and at the same time buy bread or challah from her for Shabbat.

(Page 41)

Sokher, a good friend of my father's, was also able to teach but did not have the time because he was very busy trading. He was very poor and a fidgeter[1]. He had a wife who was very rough, unlike him, who was rather petite. Besides, he had three daughters, also coarse and very fat...I usually came to his store to buy "gaz" [kerosene], candles and sugar, and brought him butter and cheese to sell. My mother could make very good cheeses, they had the reputation of being the best...

23.

Now I want to describe you a little bit the shtetl Odelsk[2]:

In the center of the shtetl there was the market, which was a large square with trampled earth to keep it dry in winter. Almost every week, on Sunday and Thursday, fairs were held there. The local Jews lived from these markets...The "goyim" [gentiles] brought wool to various homes, and the girls earned enough from its processing into stockings and socks to clothe themselves. The "goyim" in turn, both the men and the women who brought the wool, bought a little vodka to drink in the houses, and none of them came out of the house sober afterwards...

Other "goyim" came to the fair in Odelsk to buy a calf, a sheep or a horse. The "goyim" came from the surrounding villages to sell their products: Eggs, butter, poultry, cheese, rye, wheat flour for bread, peas, lentils, and anything else Jews needed...As long as they had enough money to buy, the Jews could have all these good things. However, there were many poor and sick Jews...

---

[1] "dreykop"= In primary sense, this word means "schemer"; however, I think that another meaning is meant here.

[2] Odelsk, also called "Adelsk"

The very few wealthy Jews in the shtetl were already wholesaling. They had plenty of money and made interest-bearing loans to the gentiles...The gentiles usually "borrowed" the money until after Sukkot, when the fields were harvested...But those who could not give loans to the gentiles did not do big business. In fact, there were only a few merchants who did big business, and the others had to struggle, as we did in the colony.

(Page 42)

The colonists, who had many fields to cultivate and plant, plus cows, oxen and horses, were doing well. But those who owned only a small patch of land were really poor.

In the shtetl there were several dry-goods stores. I knew them all. But those who were not able to give the gentiles goods "on borrow" could hardly make a living from it...

In Odelsk there was a large "tserkve", an Orthodox church. It stood sideways next to the market. The "goyim" flocked to the church on Sunday from all the villages in the area on the "Zubritser Way", bringing many things to sell...

The Zubritzer Way passed right by our house. We ran out and bought from the passing gentiles eggs, chickens, little calves, little sheep and spun wool... One could buy goods from us right next to our house, but many of the other [colonists] did not want to sell [locally] because they thought they would get more money for their products at the market in Odelsk.

When the "goyim" came to Odelsk, they would go to the "tserkve" to pray and then trade. Afterwards they would visit the taverns and get drunk. Almost every house in the shtetl had some liquor for sale...

Thursday was the day of the bigger fair. On that day, the market traded oxen, calves, geese and ducks...I remember a woman from our colony. When she became a widow, she moved to Odelsk and traded with earthenware vessels, with pots, jugs, bowls, plates, milk pots and other dishes. She was called *"Khayke di Teperke" (Chaike the Potter)*...She lived with an old blind woman who was called *Shoshe Merke*. She was thought to be a rich person. Her house was on a hill and I often visited her, climbing up several flights of stairs. My mother sent me to her to sell cheese and butter.

I forgot to tell you how the cheese was made. You had to put the milk in the oven for half an hour and let it simmer. The scalded cheese then had to be strained. To do this, it was placed in a linen bag. The bag was hung on a stick to drain. The liquid that trickled out,

(Page 43)

was called "sirovetke" [whey]. Then, when one wanted to process the cheese, one put it in a cheese sack between two wooden boards, one was at the bottom, the other at the top. On the upper board, heavy stones were placed and the cheese was left overnight. The next day the cheese was taken out of the sacks, salted and left to dry for a week or two...Butter was beaten from cream in a butter churn. This was very hard, you had to beat with your hands. I should have written this earlier, but I forgot.

Now let's go back to Odelsk. When there was market, I remember, many Jews stood there with their goods on the tables. Those who had even the smallest bit of goods traded at the market. From this they led a meager life, except for those who had big stores.

24.

As I wrote earlier, next to our house in the colony passed a road called "Zubritser Way". Coming from many villages, it led to Odelsk, Amdur and Grodno. As soon as you entered Odelsk on the Zubritser Way, just behind the "meshtshanes"[the more privileged citizens], came the huge store, as big as maybe a block in America. The owner's name was *Zundl*. Well, whoever went in with grain or with other products sold everything to Zundl. They did not take money but, in exchange for their products, took goods from the store and now and then they, additionally, took something on loan...

In the store there was haberdashery, cheap cloth and linen. I can't even describe what wealth was in this store...Behind the store there was a big granary with grain and also a "lidovne" [a kind of ice cellar in a deep pit]. In winter, ice was chopped in the river, which was put into the "lidovne"...During the summer, meat and dairy products, beer and wine were stored in the "lidovne". I can't write down everything that was kept there. I saw it myself, because I was there several times. But you were not allowed to go far into the depths, because then you could have frozen to death...The ice was cut into large chunks, just like they use to buy chunks of ice in America to put in the freezers...

(Page 44)

In Zundl's "lidovne" many Jews stored their products, which otherwise would have spoiled in the summer. They paid him for it...

Besides the store, he ran a tavern in a large house. There were benches and tables, and wine and liquor were sold, not only to the "goyim", but also to the Jews at feasts and weddings. When I was a little girl, I used to go there to buy everything we needed, because at Zundl you could get everything from the smallest to the largest...

Zundl's wife was called *Mekhlye [Mechlie]*, she was of small, somewhat bent stature, but a good businesswoman. In those days she could already write and calculate and helped excellently to run the business...

As for the "lidovne", I would like to add that it was dug quite deep in the earth, about 30 feet in depth and 100 feet in length. It was a big cellar, and they stored there one piece of ice on top of the other so that it would not melt...

Twenty-eight years ago, my brother Yehoshue visited me in Los Angeles before he left for San Francisco. After that he traveled to Auckland and met compatriots from Odelsk, and do you know who? Zundl's older son, Khayim Hershl and Efraim Leyke's older son. I don't remember what his name was. He also met Sokher's son *Gershon*, who had a hardware store in Auckland. My brother worked for Gershon for two years and then left for New York.

25.

As I have told before, many from our colony who had little land left for Bialystok to work either in weaving or in the dyeworks. The little land they owned they leased to gentiles who worked it "half on half," that is, they kept one half of the grain ready for harvest themselves and the other half was given to the owner of the field. Those who worked in Bialystok used to come home to the colony for Passover and Sukkot

(Page 45)

In the colony there were also people who not only owned a little piece of land, but were also craftsmen, like *Kalman Abe*. Kalman was a blacksmith; he had a forge and made knives. On Monday his wife *Reyzke* went to Sokółka to sell some of his knives, on Tuesday she sold knives in Krynki and on Thursday in Amdur. Kalman had very little land, which he leased to a gentile for two years. He built a small house with a forge and bought a cow, and so he toiled away...

Or, let's take *Moyshe Khayim*, the son of *Khayke di Teperke (the Potter)*. He [Moyshe] had learned the trade of cabinetmaker in Sokółka, and after that he married his uncle's daughter, *Rokhel [Rachel] Itke*, in the colony. He got his late father's field, which his uncle used to work, built his own little house, bought a few cows, and the profit he made from the field and from the cabinetmaking let him live a nice life...

Let us tell about *Velvel Leyzer*, the brother of Khayke di Teperke's husband. He was a village tailor. His older boy was called *Yakev-Shiye*. Velvel taught him tailoring, and then he and his son, Yakev Shiye went about the villages sewing in the houses of the gentiles. Friday night, however, they came home to the colony for Shabbat.

Rokhel Itke, the daughter of the tailor Velvel Leyzer, who married Moyshe Khayim, the son of Khayke di Teperke (the Potter), was my friend. We went together to the pastures and tended the cattle.

Concerning the colony, I want to mention that many families intermarried, and most of them were related to each other...

26.

And now I come back to *Sokher*, who was also called *Sokher-Arye*. He had no money of his own to trade, but had to borrow money. Later, he had to pay back the loan and borrow new money. In this way, he toiled away.

(Page 46)

When he bought the grain to sell in Grodno, he always came to my father and instructed him to drive the grain to Grodno with his horse and wagon and to bring other things from Grodno, such as barrels of herring and kerosene and sacks of salt, sugar and flour.

In the process, it once happened on a dark night, when my father was returning from Grodno on the snowy road in a great frost, that the wagon overturned in a large pit... My father had to wait until it became day, and when it was light, he realized that he was not on the right path. There was no one here to help him lift the goods out of the pit. He had to struggle with it alone, and by the time he had loaded everything back onto the wagon, the little horse was so frozen and hungry that it wouldn't budge from the place...

My poor father, what could he do? He had to push the cart along with the horse, he had to manage everything all by himself. Now he was a very strong man. When the gentiles wanted to harm the Jews and graze their rye or wheat, my father raised such a shout from afar that the gentiles fled like poisoned mice.

But that night, when the wagon overturned, my father became very ill and got "plyurasi" [pleurisy], that is, he had water in his lungs. The feldsher, a good man, could not help him. Maybe if they had looked [for a doctor] immediately, they could have helped him, but it was missed. There was a good doctor in Krynki, but he took a lot of money for a visit. Finally, my mother went with my father to Grodno. There was a hospital there, but the doctors there would not keep him more than a few days without payment. My mother brought him home as a sick man...We had no money to hire a person to plow the field, so my father went to plow himself.

My father was getting sicker and sicker, but he didn't want to admit that he was so sick. He jumped out of bed, ran to the barn to thresh out some rye so that a little bread could be baked for the children. The rye had to be ground into flour, which had to be carried to the mill, which was a mile away...

(Page 47)

I remember how my mom and I carried the grain to the mill in two sacks, half of it me, the other half my mother. It was a windmill, where the rye, wheat, barley and also buckwheat were ground; the barley became barley pearls, the wheat became white flour, from which the challah was baked on Shabbat and "lokshn un farfl" [egg noodles with egg barley] was prepared.

My brother Yehoshue was a boy of 14 at that time. When my father could no longer thresh by himself, he took my brother to the barn. The latter had no warm clothes to wear, so unfortunately he always arrived at the barn completely frozen. However, as soon as he started to thresh with the flail, he quickly became warm...

The barn was far from our house, in America it would be "a block", so during big snowstorms you had to walk through the snow up to your knee. When you got back to the apartment afterwards, it was very cold there. We had no money to buy wood. You had to buy wood in the fall, because you couldn't get any in the winter. We heated with straw; for this we tied the straw in big bundles so that the heat was kept a little...You can understand the value of the warmth of straw...In the past, when my father was still earning money, my mother would go to the forest with the "goyim" and buy birch wood, because this keeps the heat well...After buying birch wood, it was necessary to let it dry. Pine wood was also bought, when it dried it was a pleasure to heat with it. However, it did not keep the heat, you also had to have birch wood and mix it with pine wood...

Sometimes we bought peat. Peat kept the heat very long, but it stank a lot. If you did not plaster the stove, you could not sit in the house without harming yourself. The peat also had to dry and be bought in the summer...We could do all this when my father was healthy and earning money. When he fell ill, our serious worries began; sickness, hunger and cold, and so many problems...

(Page 48)

In the summer it was still bearable. We had three cows, which we milked in the summer, we sold the milk products in Odelsk and bought a few pounds of bread from Yehoshue the baker. If we only brought one piece of fresh bread, it was already much too little. Before you knew it, there was nothing left.

If it was a good potato year, we thanked God for His grace. Early in the morning we had boiled potatoes for the children, potatoes for lunch, and potatoes for dinner. And we praised and thanked the "oybershtn" [the Lord].

As you already know, the children were not given any dairy products. Neither milk, God forbid, nor butter, nor cheese, nor sour milk. Only the "sirovetke", the whey, could be drunk, after the sour milk had been boiled. Cheese was also made from the whey, and only that was given to the children to eat...What else could our parents do, because from the few milk products they had to buy bread and other things, for example, shoes, a bit of linen or a shirt to wear on the body. One needed two shirts for each child, nothing from good, but from coarse linen, but in any case one needed a shirt! And now you can imagine why our parents did not give us children the cheese and butter to eat...

27.

When we had better times, my mother bought a big jug of syrup; and a piece of bread with syrup was very tasty! Mom also greased pieces of bread with cream for us, but that was already a feast for us! In better times, parents worried about us and fed us well...Our small piece of land was well cultivated. Father plowed and sowed alone, and it was successful for us. We had only a small field, but we got more out of it than those who had a lot of land. Since our field was so fertile, we were able to keep more livestock...

In better times we had wood stored for the

(Page 49)

whole winter, and it was warm... I remember that while my father was in Bialystok, my mother hired gentiles to go into the forest and buy ten loads of wood. After that, she hired gentiles again to chop the wood and pile it up so that it would dry.

But that winter, when my father was sick, we suffered greatly from the cold...Not far from the colony was a forest where the poor people went and collected wood chips. These shavings kept the heat well, because they had a lot of bark...They called this forest "Zubritser Wood".

In better times, my parents had a lot of animals and through them manure to fertilize the field. I mean the waste of the cattle. By fertilizing the field they had a lot of grain...I remember that we had only one third of a "field number", but we had more yield than those who had half a number. Even from a distance you could see how fertile our field was...

When times were better, my mother ordered a very beautiful dress for me from the ladies' tailor in Sokółka. All the girls envied me for it. I still remember the color of the dress, it was green. And it was sewn at the bottom like with a tunic over it, and there was a pad sewn in so that the dress flared out from the bottom. It was a very beautiful dress! I remember that on Rosh Hashanah we girls went to the synagogue to hear the blowing of the shofar and the girls could not take their eyes off my dress...

My father was very good to me, as was my mother. In the summer I cut the grain, and I was a very fast reaper. I cut for two reapers. My father, I remember, would come riding to me on his horse at noon to bring me dry cheeses we had prepared and sliced to take to the field. My father loved me very much, I was his only daughter at that time. Many years later another girl was born, but by then I was already grown up...

When we had cut our grain in the field, I went to neighbors and earned 50 kopecks a day. Others received 45 kopecks a day. But I finished the bed I was cutting

(Page 50)

much earlier, so the other reapers had to hurry because of me. They were angry with me, and they were right! Today I know that there was wrong of me, but who understood it then? I was young and strong and I could prove myself...

28.

I think that my best years were when I was 12 to 14 years old. Also in our home these were the best years...My mother prepared the most beautiful Shabbat, she baked challah, braided bun ornaments, and this was sufficient for the children for a whole week. However, I did not let my mother knead the dough in the kneading trough, but did it myself...The dough was made from three pood [49 kg] of grain...Do you know why I was so strong? We had a cellar where we stored potatoes in the winter and dairy products in the summer. And I had a sweet tooth. And when my mother went away with the cattle behind the house to graze, leaving me with the little children, I would go down into the cellar. The cellar was very deep, and there was a big ladder there. You had to be careful when you went down. In the glass that I had taken down from the apartment, I filled a little cream from each milk jug and drank my fill...Good for me when the children had fallen asleep, but [once], when they started to cry and my mother heard this, she came running, held me by the cheeks and pinched them in such a way that they were swollen for quite a few days...

I was 10 years old at the time and should have known that you can't skim cream, because then there's none left, and you can't make butter either. My father was very angry with my mother for making my cheeks that swollen. My good father said that the little bit of cream would not make us poor, I am a good child and work a lot given my young age, and for such a little thing you still make a child of 10 years swollen cheeks!...

(Page 51)

So that was how it was, that was the life we had to lead. And maybe my mother was really right. I loved to snack when mom went away and left me alone with the kids...

I come back to my father now, when he was driving back from Grodno, his cart with the goods overturned and he got sick...He didn't want to admit that he was sick. He said: "A strong man like me is supposed to be sick?! Am I supposed to admit that such a little thing as hauling a bit of merchandise out of the pit made me sick? No!"

Not far from us was a piece of land called "Balenitsa" [or "Baletsina" or later it is called "Byaleshtsine"]. This was a very large field overgrown with grass, and everyone from the colony left their cattle there to graze, even the horses were taken there to remain for a whole night. Around the "Balenitsa" there was a piece of land where rye was planted. It had to be fenced, because one didn't want the horses grazing on the "Balenitsa" to get to the cornfield at night, to crop it and trample...My father went to the "Balenitsa" and dug a pit around our bed [which was also adjacent there] so that the horses could not get in and eat the grain. After that, our great misfortune happened. It was a very hot day and my father was very thirsty from the heat, he was very sweaty and drank cold water...soon he got pneumonia...

I don't remember how long he was sick. But I remember how my mother took him to Grodno to the "hekdesh", here in America they would call it "county hospital". In the "hekdesh" he did not recover, so he came home again, lay down in bed, his body was swollen, and he was getting worse and worse. My mother took him to the "hekdesh" once again. There were already such strong frosts that one would not have driven out even a dog out of pity. In such a frost, my mother took him to the "hekdesh" and left me with the children in the house...At home there was not the smallest piece of wood. Only a little milk supply was there, so I made some cheese, churned a few pounds of butter and went away to Odelsk to sell the few pounds of butter and the cheese, because I wanted to load my handcart

(Page 52)

with wood to warm the poor children and I had to buy a piece of bread from the baker...

The frost was burning, the snow was so deep, and I could no longer see a path. There was no big road here. One had to look for the way. I was walking towards "kidesh hashem", my martyrdom. I got lost. I was completely frozen...In the colony, you didn't wear "bloomers," as they say in America, only open underpants. There were no galoshes either. You thanked God if you had gaiters, that is, shoes. I didn't have a warm coat either. I barely managed to drag myself home, [once there,] I had to sit down and dip my feet and hands in cold water. If I had held my frozen feet and hands in warm water, it would have pierced me as if with needles ...At least I was able to bring a few pounds of bread for the children. I had to borrow the bread from *Moyshe-Shiye the Baker* in Odelsk. For the cheese and butter I sold, I only got a cart full of wood to buy.

When my father came from Grodno the second time, he knew that he would not live much longer. His body was so swollen that I could not recognize him at all. We kissed, this was the last time. After that I never kissed my good father again...He was such a handsome man, my father, a tall, blond, with rosy cheeks and with a long blond beard...

My father came back from Grodno on Shabbat Rosh Chodesh. He agonized until the 15th day of the month of Iyar before he passed away. May his soul peacefully rest in Gan Eden. This happened 67 years ago. I, the author, was 18 years old at that time. When he died, he was only 49 years old and left behind six children...My father was a very smart man. They later changed his name *Leybe* to *Leybeshke*, and when one of our children said something clever, there was a saying that he "has Leybershke's head on him".

In our colony we could not get a "minyen" [prayer quorum] to say the Kaddish prayer for our good father. Therefore, Notke and Alter ran to Odelsk to say the Kaddish...My brother Alter was not yet nine years old, and my brother Note was seven.

(Page 53)

29.

When my father was sick, we needed the feldsher, but every time he came, we had to pay him. Since we had no money, we sold the grain...When our father died, there was nothing left for the little children to eat. There was still father's family, but we were always angry with each other...A good "goy" [gentile] brought a wagon full of flour for bread, barley for pearl barley, peas, lentils, and potatoes, and gave it all to my mother. Three years ago, my brother Yehoshue [Ishye] was my guest in Los Angeles and told me about that good "goy". The produce that the good gentile brought, my mother used for the children until we could harvest the new grain from the fields...

When my father was so sick, I already had a little work in Bialystok and was allowed to prepare the warp yarn tapes here and there. But when my father became very ill, my mother wrote to me that I had to come home and take care of the little children. My mother had to go with Dad to doctors in Grodno...Later, when she brought Dad back from Grodno, I consulted with her and we decided that I should go back to Bialystok...

Shortly after Passover I left for Bialystok. All my life, I have been saddened by the fact that I left home and was not with my father when he died...Everyone from our colony who worked in Bialystok knew that my father was dead, but no one wanted to tell me...I went home to Shavuot...Inside I somehow felt that my father was no longer alive...One went from Bialystok to Sokółka by train, and from Sokółka one took the horse cart. All our colonists who worked in Bialystok usually went home to Shavuot...One had to pay 25 kopecks per person to go by horse cart from Sokólka to the colony. The poor walked on foot. I also had to walk...When we were already not far from home, only about a vyorst (about 1 km) away,

(Page 54)

where the village of Vonyevits [Wojnowce?] is located, I asked the gentiles I knew there, but they didn't want to tell me the truth either...

When I was already approaching our field and began to walk on the furrow, I knew that my father was no longer alive, because the field (which was called "place") revealed it to me by its condition. I saw that the rye was overgrown with wild grasses and I understood that my father is no longer in this world...

I entered our house and mom instructed me to sit "shiva" for one hour. If it has been more than a month since someone passed away, the close relatives only need to sit "shiva" for one day, if it has been less than a month, one needs to sit for seven days. I cried and lamented for over two years, but, what is covered by the earth must be forgotten...

Oh indeed, it was very painful for us. We were a big family with six children, and two boys, Note and Alter, already had to go to the cheder...My brother Yehoshue [Ishye] learned in the Bialystoker Bes-Medresh [house of study]. Usually rich Jews prayed in this Bes-Medresh. They took a liking to Ishye and declared him a sub-shames. He studied, supported the shames and earned a few rubles...I forgot that it was actually not a Bes-Medresh at all, but a large "shul" [synagogue] called "The Shul". It was located on Yureftser Gas [Jurowiecka Street].

Excerpt of an old map, courtesy of Dr. Tomek Wisniewski. We can see Sokółka, Wojnowce, Wielka Zubrzyca, Isaaka and Odelsk.

I remember when my brother and I came home for Passover to visit Mom with the children. Mother had prepared matzos, wine, and meat – everything you had to have for Passover. Passover had to be celebrated; if a family didn't have anything for Passover, produce from the city had to be brought in. You wonder why I write so much about Passover? Because Passover was the holiest of holidays...

Then, when Mother prepared the table for the Seder, a loud crying arose in the house, and everything remained standing on the table. The wine goblets, the food, nothing was touched, everyone in the house was filled with grief. Thus passed several Passover feasts...My brother and I also went home for Sukkot, so as not to wander around in a foreign country. So we came to the colony to see our poor mother with her poor

children, the little orphans...so we mourned for over two, three years...

(Page 55)

30.

I made friends in Bialystok with a girl, her name was *Peshe* and she was really a good girl. She was a spooler and worked at *Preyzman* [1] on Yureftser Gas [Jurowiecka Street]. Preyzman was a very big manufacturer. She interceded for me with the master of the factory, and he told her to call me. So she came to me with such joyful news that I had a job and no longer had to move from one factory to another to find a job as a warper.

The master hired me and I received three rubles a week. I prepared the warp yarn tapes, and if there was not enough to warp, I repaired the pieces of cloth. I was as well off as one could be. I could send mother with the children a few rubles...Three rubles a week, that was a big income! The winders earned no more than one and a half rubles a week. A warper could earn even more, you could work your way up to six rubles a week...

In the factory there were 60 looms and two "leyketnikes" [foremen, masters]. I worked in Preyzman's factory for a long time. After that I went to *Leyzer Endler*. At Leyzer Endler I already received four rubles a week.

If you were a warper at Leyzer Endler, it meant that you were the best warper in town. However, I didn't stay with him long, maybe a year, then I was called back to Preyzman...One of the foremen of Preyzman, *Yude Khatseles*, asked my brother Ishye to get me away from Leyzer Endler.

At Preyzman I was already earning four and a half rubles a week...And when it was "bizi" [busy], as they say in America, there was still a warp yarn tape to prepare after work. For such a warp you got 60 kopeks, and so I could help my mom and the children...

---

[1] see   https://www.jewishbialystok.pl/Prejsman-Preisman-Prejsman-.L.-,5404,4334

Immediately after my father's death, however, I was in a very bad way, I had nothing to eat and not even the 50 kopecks to pay for my room...A warper had to be well dressed, but from what could I have dressed myself? I still had no work, and when, with great effort, I finally got some work, I had to spend the money on food. My brother Yehoshue [Ishye] was studying in shul,

(Page 56)

and when he was hungry, he would put up at my place. I would cook dinner for my brother and me...The landlady was a good person and instructed me to make Shabbath with my brother; from time to time she would lend me money until I earned some myself...

Unfortunately, my brother had to freeze in winter because he wore only a thin jacket, short pants and torn shoes. It was heartbreaking to look at him...He was a tall, handsome and very smart person...And when he came to me, so as not to starve, I cooked some barley soup, bound with a little milk, and bought a herring, which I cut into pieces for quite a few days...

31.

A few months after my father's death, my little brother died. You can certainly imagine what happened there. I wasn't at home; my brother Ishye and I were in Bialystok and we had to starve ourselves. Despite all this, as I earned just a little, I sent some of it to my mother...

At that time, a famine broke out in our colony. It was in the second year after my father's death. The grain in the fields had burned, and there was nothing left for the colonists to eat...The government issued corn, but not enough, so there was great hunger in my mother's house...My sister Sheyne Gitl, a child of four, my brother Alter, in his tenth year, and my brother Note, in his seventh year, unfortunately had to eat grass...My sister Sheyne Gitl is now a wealthy woman, you can say she is rich, and she still to this day happily tells of that time when she and the two brothers ate grass...

The two brothers died a long time ago at a young age.

I now return to the time after my father's death. It had already been a year since his death, so the brothers no longer had to say Kaddish. My mother brought my younger brother, Notke, to Grodno, to study in the

(Page 57)

"talmetoyre" [free religious community school]. Many members of my mother's family lived in Grodno. She visited them and told them about her late husband and that she did not know what to do, because everything had been spent due to her husband's illness. She said that she had brought her boy Notke to Grodno to study. He was now eight years old, and she asked her family to take care of him. He was still so young, she said, and she could not leave him alone. Her family should please take care that he, God forbid, does not suffer hunger and does not become a bad boy. She organized for him "esn teg" [daytime eating of poor students by rich people or relatives], but not for all days...

One of them, a cousin of my mother, took on the duty of feeding Notke three days a week and making sure that he lacked nothing...This cousin's name was *Avrohem Berl*; he was the finest man in the world. In fact, he was a water-carrier. He owned a horse and wagon and assisted strangers who brought and distributed water. He was so beautiful that it was a pleasure to look at him, and he was a good man, a benefactor. He had his own house, and in addition, houses that he rented out...And when he drove around with the water and came across Notke, who was just going to study in the "talmetoyre", he never forgot to call him over, ask if he had anything to eat, and give him ten kopecks... But my brother was ashamed and did not tell him the truth that he had no food for a day or two...

His wife was called *Peshe*. She was a tall and beautiful person, and such a good one as I had never met before. When I had no work and came to Grodno, her door was always open. She was so kind-hearted that I almost did not want to go to any other one of my family...

Peshe and Avrohem Berl had three children, two girls and a boy. He also had two brothers, one was a soldier, a very handsome man who was soon to return from military service. I have forgotten what his name was. I remember that he was the second brother of Avrohem Berl, the third was called *Yehoshue (Ishye)*, he was a bricklayer and made a lot of money. Avrohem Berl took care of his two brothers when their parents died very young... My brother

(Page 58)

Notke learned a few years in Grodno, I don't remember how many...Notke was scrawny and weak all his life, he had starved too much in his childhood...

32.

Now I will write what happened to my brother Ishye. He was eager to do an apprenticeship as a weaver, but for that you had to pay a hundred rubles. As you know, he was a sub-shames and received food one day a week from a well-to-do gentleman who was fond of him. His name was *Avrohem Tseyteles* and he was a "leynketnik" [foreman, master] in the weaving factory. My brother asked Avrohem Tseyteles to teach him how to weave. [The latter asked him:]

"Do you have any money? You have to pay 100 rubles!"

But my brother replied:

"If I had 100 rubles, I would be a rich man and would not even speak to you, but would become a manufacturer myself!"

Avrohem Tseyteles laughed, took him in the factory and taught him to weave. Later, when he was already working as a weaver, he paid off the 100 rubles. My brother worked for him for a long time. However, he did not earn much, because when you learn to weave cloth, you have to be very careful, and if you make a mistake in the cloth you weave, you have to pay for it. Also, he didn't work fast, so he didn't earn enough to help mother out with the children.

I have already written that my mother was so hungry that the two little children ate the grass in the street. My brother and I did not know about this. My mother did not want to inform us, so as not to cause us so much grief... Often, I went without eating enough to send a few rubles to mother with the children...

I have told you before that there was a great drought in the colony. Even the cows did not have enough to eat and were emaciated, mooing for nights because of hunger. And since they were hungry, they did not give milk. I had already written

(Page 59)

before that they made butter and cheese from the milk and sold the products to maintain the house. However, now, when the great calamity of drought came upon us, mother did not know what to do at all...The disaster affected all the colonists, but my mother, the young widow with the little orphans, it hit more than the others. The children were miserable, had nothing to wear, no shirts on their bodies, no shoes on their feet, no warm long jackets to put on. So they toiled without a father for three years until I found a good factory and could work as a warper...

My brother Ishye taught my brother Alter how to weave cloth from which to sew long jackets, that is, he taught him the craft of a weaver. And do you know how old my brother Alter was at that time? Not older than 13 or 14 years, that's how young he was! But, what was to be done? It was just fortunate that he was a tall one with broad shoulders, so he looked like an 18-year-old young man. Therefore, my brother Ishye could take him into the factory and train him. Alter even became a better weaver than my brother Ishye.

33.

And when my two brothers and I were already working, we all felt a little better...We were even beginning to think about how we could manage to get Mom, the kids, Notke and my little sister Gitl to Bialystok.

My brother Ishye taught his brother Notke, who was then 13 years old, to weave. And the latter was gifted and became a good weaver...Notke was a small boy and looked much younger than his age. Why was that? I have already written why: he was parched with hunger. When he studied in Grodno, he lacked a few days in the week when food was organized for him, but he did not want to say so and was ashamed to ask to get food on the other days as well...He got used to not eating anything...In the colony there was grass, but in Grodno the streets were paved, there was no grass growing for him...

(Page 60)

When an inspector appeared at the factory to check if everything was all right, my brother Ishye used to hide Notke under the loom, because he was still too young to work...Notke could not yet work alone on a loom. For a long time he worked together with his brother Ishye on one loom, until he grew older and taller...

We had to go through a lot of suffering, and I really don't know how we endured it all...

34.

Now I'm writing down what I forgot before:

It was right in the summer after my father died. Not far from us was a large field called "Byaleshtsine". In the middle of the field there was an area where grass grew. Around this meadow grew rye, wheat and other grains...one let the grass grow all summer long and cut it only in the month of Ov [July-August], so that one had something for the cattle all winter. The meadow was called "Minketsner fields" because it bordered directly on the village of Minketse [Miszlkieniki?]...

From the mentioned "Byaleshtsine" there passed another piece of meadow, like a narrow belt. It was a little bit divided and it was called "Shmole Blotkes" [narrow swamp]. In its center was a valley with a small river running through it. Grass grew on both sides of the river, and this was cut at the same time as the rest of the grass on the "Byaleshtsine". Why do you think I am writing about these meadows? Because at that time my mother went to cut the rye and took my little sister to the field. It was very hot and my mother bathed her in the river. But soon, a disaster happened...My sister's whole body was covered with wounds, even her face and ears...I remember when I came home for Sukkot with my brother Ishye, my sister was lying there very sick and the wounds were causing her great pain...My sister was three and a half years old at that time...

In our colony there was an old, very pious Jew who always asked for money for challah on Friday. His name was *Dovid*

(Page 61)

Leyzer… My little sister was lying on the big stove at that time and said to old Dovid Leyzer that her wounds hurt so much that she couldn't stand it anymore...On that he said to her: "I am already an old man, and when I have died, your Mom shall bring you to me and stroke your whole body with my dead hand"...

The illness lasted for a long time, more than a few weeks, and when Reb Dovid Leyzer died, they actually brought my sister in his family's house...At first the family refused a little, but when Mother told them that Dovid Leyzer himself had promised, the family agreed. The dead man's hand was stroked over my sister's body and she got well. May his soul shine brightly in Gan Eden...

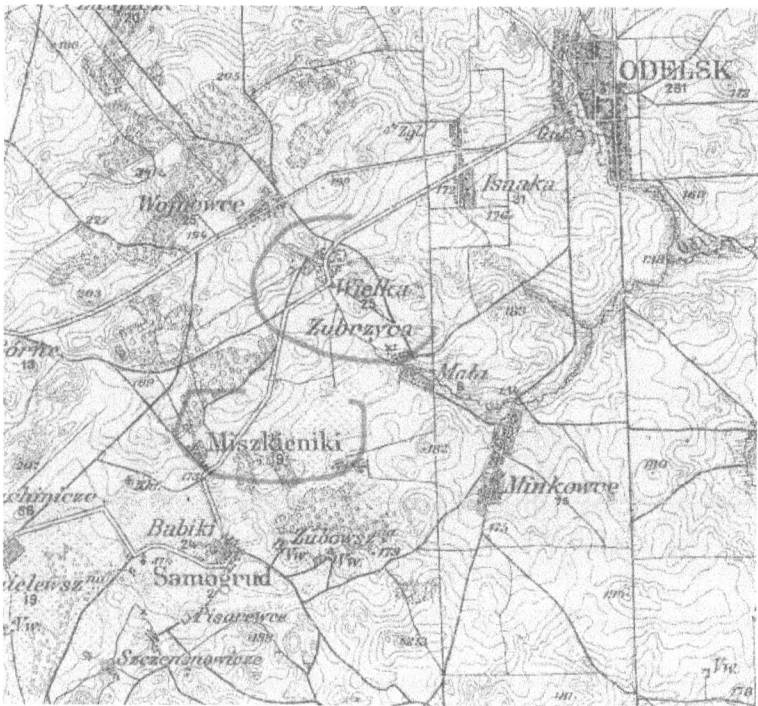

Old map: courtesy of Dr.Tomek Wisniewski, colony Isaaka (Izakova, Zakova), Wielka Zubrzyca (Zubritz), Odelsk and Sokółka

35.

I forgot to write that when my little sister was three months old, my mother had to go to the cornfield to harvest and couldn't take the baby with her to the field...She left it to my brother, Alter. He was not yet eight years old and was supposed to take care of the baby. However, he had to bring the baby to Mom in the field twice a day for breastfeeding...After all, the child should not die of thirst and with Mom the milk should not dry up...He had to take the baby very far to the "Skroblyesk fields", more than two kilometers from home...What happened? My brother Alter swaddled the baby in wraps and put her in a pillow. He set off with the pillow to the fields...When he arrived at Mom's, she took the pillow from him, but, oy vey! The child was not there! What a great fright! It was started to look for the baby, and indeed it was found on the way where my brother had gone...That was a joy and happiness!

I should have written this earlier, but I had forgotten...I also forgot to write that the river in "Shmole Blotkes", in which my mother had bathed my little sister, had the fame

(Page 62)

that there were devils in it... I remember when I was not yet a big girl, we, that is a group of girls, used to pick berries in "Shmole Blotkes". We were afraid to lag behind the others, lest some devil should catch us...

When my sister Sheyne Gitl recovered from the skin rash that had affected her in that river, she became a beautiful girl again. I can say that she was really a little hero, a child with such problems who had no food and had to eat grass, as I wrote, and yet she grew up as a beauty...

36.

Now, I will begin with a new story from our lives:

My situation had already improved somewhat. I worked at Preyzman in a good factory and was already earning three rubles a week...I sent my mother as much money as I could. Three rubles was not much, but I myself was extremely thrifty in order to be able to help at home and cause mother and my little sister to live better...

I remember seeing rich children walking, dressed in embroidered costumes, like the Russians wore: a red long blouse, embroidered with beautiful flowers and a "spudnitse", a skirt, what they call "skirt" here [in America]. The "spudnitse" was a navy blue color, and over it was a white apron, also embroidered with beautiful flowers [1] . When I brought something like that to my little sister on the holiday, it suited her so well...I used to embroider that at night, because I didn't have time during the day. The embroidery I managed very well and in the colony it was a big surprise, because there you did not see such costumes, however, quite in Odelsk...There were officers quartered in Odelsk and their children used to wear such costumes...

I wrote before that my brothers had been trained as weavers. They were still very young and slept

(Page 63)

in the factory where they worked. I used to go to the factory to collect their laundry (which we called "gret" in Bialystok). I washed out their shirts, underpants and socks, and darned the socks so that there was no need to buy new ones...

In the factory where I worked there was a "parovke" (a machine driven by steam). At 12 o'clock the "parovke" turned itself off, because the workers had to eat lunch. We girls had an hour to eat and rest until the "parovke" started up again...During the hour lunch break I washed my brothers' clothes. There was water heated by the "parovke", and the water already had soap in it. I was not the only one who washed, other girls did it too...and at home, in my quarters, I ironed...

I sewed for me a beautiful "spudnitse" [skirt] with beautiful stripes, white and red, and the "spudnitse" was pleated, like today's "skirts". I also sewed for myself a beautiful blouse made of red cloth. It looked so beautiful, it caught everyone's eye... "Morey" cost a lot, it was included in flowers. And my dress was decorated almost everywhere with "morey"... I love to go beautifully dressed.

---

[1] A little mental leap follows; apparently Rachel sewed such a costume for her sister

I remember when a new style, fashion came out, black "tepetene" dresses[1] that I immediately sewed up...The dress was decorated with a lot of "morey" [moire].

In those days, when you could make things cheaply, it cost me already 25 rubles...

When our place of residence was still in the colony, we went home to Mom for Sukkot. I remember what was going on regarding the expensive dress I had sewn. No one in the colony had ever worn such a beautiful dress...

Shortly after Sukkot I went back to work in Bialystok. I left the dress with my mother. After a few months, on Friday, I went to the colony during the day especially because of my beautiful dress, and do you know why? A girl from the factory was celebrating a wedding! I had had some beautiful dresses with me, but not such a beautiful one, which I had left with my mother. It really was the most beautiful dress at the wedding...

In a year or two, other fashions came out. People

(Page 64)

wore gray dresses with velvet sleeves. In the place where I lived, there were also rich people whose daughters wore gray dresses with velvet sleeves. Just as I saw it, I also had such a gray dress with velvet sleeves...

I had it very nicely finished and it looked very good on me. I was not fat and had a slim waist. That's why girls liked to be friends with me and they thought I was very educated. I was not a scholar. However, I could pray and read a Yiddish-language newspaper well. Also, I could write a little Russian and read a Russian book - not really well, but I understood and knew what it was about.

On Shabbat, all of us girls went for a walk on "Varshever Gas" [Warszawska Street]. I remember that I wore a beautiful jacket made of plush. I had bought the plush in the office of my factory owner on installments.

_____
[1] I think that with "tepetene" dresses the author may have meant taffeta dresses. Dresses made of taffeta, moire and metal sequins were high fashion in the 19th century.

I gave it to a ladies tailor to sew the jacket. It was a kind of three-quarter length coat.

With it, I wore a white hat made of plush, like a man's hat. I also wore boots, and on Shabbat evening, when I went for a walk with my girlfriends, I had so much fun!

I often went for walks with my brother Ishye, and what fun it was! The frost was burning and the snow was pouring...

37.

Next to the place where I lived was a store, something like a grocery in America, and I bought everything from them. There was a room available and my landlady suggested that I take it for myself and my brothers. That's what happened. I actually took the room. The landlords had a maid who cooked dinner for us. I already prepared it and the maid cooked the best dinner out of it, so my brothers livened up...They didn't have to sleep in the factory anymore...

We lived with these people for more than a year. They were very good, learned and rich people... However, it came about that they sold

(Page 65)

their store and we had to move out of their place. We lived at that time on Yureftser Gas [Jurowiecka Street] next to Bialystoktsek [Bialystoczek]. On the same street was also the factory where I worked, and it was such a pity about the good room and such good people...But I could not change it and had to go and look for another room. We were four people after all and needed a big room, and besides, we needed someone to cook for us...

Old Bialystok Map, excerpt, courtesy of Dr. Tomek Wisniewski

We were offered a room with a family that was not rich. The man was old and could not earn much. His name was *Itsi Yankel*. His wife was called *Rokhel [Rachel] Itsi Yankel's*. They had four daughters. Two were already married. One was named *Dina* and her husband *Berl*. He was a plumber, but was sick and could not earn a living, so the poor mother supported them. You wonder what the mother did? Well, she used to go to rich families and cook, and sometimes she went to maternity wards to take care.

The parents took more pleasure in the second daughter. She was called *Sheyne Bashke*, and her husband was called *Yisroel*. He was a dressmaker and sewed dresses for rich women...As soon as a new fashion came out, he was the first to offer it...He had quite a few girls working for him as tailors. He was very good to his wife's parents, better than a son of their own, and they boasted of their good son-in-law.

The third daughter was called *Dreyne*. She worked as a "nuperke" and although not tall, she was smart and beautiful. She was still unmarried. I worked with Dreyne in the Leyzer Endler factory, she as a "nuperke" and I as a "warper".

The fourth daughter was still a young girl of 16, but already a seamstress. She had done this apprenticeship with her brother-in-law...You wonder why I am describing this family? Because it has a lot to do with me and my brother Ishye, but I will write that a little later...

Rokhl Itsi Yankel's, with whom we stayed, usually bought

(Page 66)

food for me and my brothers, which I prepared before she cooked it for us. We were fine with them too...

From time to time, a young man came to our house . He could write Yiddish, Polish and beautiful Russian. He was coming from military service and had no job, so they let him give a few Yiddish lessons, for which he got about twenty rubles a month...I noticed that he followed me when I came home from work. As soon as I entered the house, he also came in. My landlady introduced me to him, but I didn't take any interest in him because I didn't have time. My brothers would eventually come for dinner, and I had to prepare it. So I didn't talk to the man at all, and he didn't talk to me. He was talking to the landlady's young daughter. I didn't care who he was. I had my own things to get. This probably annoyed him very much, and he disappeared...

The landlady asked me afterwards how I liked the young man. I asked her what that had to do with me. Then she told me that she wanted to talk to me about a marital union...I answered her that I didn't know if I was interested. She didn't say anything more.

In the middle of the week he came to her again and the landlady told him that she had a daughter. Her name was Dina and she lived in the "Novi" [Nowy Świat], and she had a "sod" there. (A "sod" means a garden where fruits grow: apples, pears, plums, gooseberries, grapes, cherries and so on. Summer is garden season, because this is also the harvest time of the fruits: Tamez, Ov, Elul. In these months, on Shabbat, people walked in the gardens, both the girls and the young boys). The landlady agreed with the young man that he should come to her daughter in the garden on Shabbat afternoon, and that he would meet me there. (There was also a pavilion in the garden. In the parlor of the pavilion one dined on fruits and drank soda water. They used to draw it from a syphon, just as in America they draw soda water in a candy-store.) When the landlady said to me that I should come to her daughter's garden on Shabbat afternoon to meet the young man in the pavilion, I replied to her why didn't he ask me personally to go with him to the garden? In fact, I did not go...

(Page 67)

38.

Now I'll tell you what had happened to me three or four years before. I remembered only now, when I wrote about the garden...In Bialystok there was an outbreak of cholera, a plague. People were dropping like flies. At that time I was already working at Preyzman's factory. I stayed in a room not far from Varshever Gas [Warszawska Street]. My landlady maintained a garden and asked me to come to the garden on Shabbat afternoon, she said to me:

"Why do you have to hang around alone in the parlor all day, come to the garden instead!"

I actually felt melancholy in the house. I knew places in gardens where I could have gone, but I didn't because of the fear of going to someone's house because of cholera. Now that there was nowhere to go, I went into the garden and ate my fill of gooseberries and some other stuff. And, what do you think happened? Shortly after I came home, I got cholera...

When they took me in the "barak" on Shabbat evening, I was more dead than alive. I remember people standing there talking: "Alas, a miserable girl, they will soon get rid of her". Because, if you were taken in by the "barak", you didn't come out alive again...

A "barak" meant a hospital. On Gumyan Gas [Gumienna Street], the city had seized a large building. It was huge, as big as the "County Hospital" in Los Angeles. People were brought to this "barak" from all over the city, rich or poor. People who were sick with cholera were not allowed to stay at home, because they would catch it from each other.

Those who died were doused with lime and immediately burned in the yard...There was great mourning in the town. No one from the family was allowed to come to the "barak" to visit a sick person, because the whole family could get infected. Some were burned in their houses...It was indeed such a bad plague as may never hit you in your life...

I, Ishye and Alter were in Bialystok. My brother Alter was still a boy of fourteen.

(Page 68)

My brother Ishye sent him to the colony to stay at home with our little sister, while my mother should come to visit me as soon as possible, if I would stay alive…The very next day my mother came to visit, but she was not allowed to come in to see me…

My brother knew the doctors, and they let him into the "barak" on the condition that he help out there…My brother worked all night in the hospital with other sick people to watch over me. He took care of me and I stayed alive! There was another girl lying with me, her name was *Roze* and she was also one of those who were saved. She came from the Polish shtetl Pruzene [Pruzhany] and was an orphan who worked as a maid in Bialystok.

A week later, my mother was already let in to me. It was a Friday, and Mom had to go home again, because after all my little sister was there alone with my brother Alter…

I was in the "barak" for two weeks and I remember how my brother led me by the hand when I was let out so I wouldn't fall down. The people who were standing in the street and saw my brother leading me by the hand were surprised, because, as I said before, if someone with cholera was admitted to the "barak", he did not come out of there alive…

Now I will tell what antidote was taken to stop the cholera: The city took a poor young man, an orphan, and a poor girl, an orphan, and married them in the Jewish cemetery, and in the Bote-Medroshim [study-houses] they recited psalms…After a few months the cholera came to a halt…

39.

We lived with Rokhl Itsi-Yankel's for a few years. Meanwhile, our mother in the colony was not well. My father's brother was causing her great grief. His name was *Artshik*. Artshik

(Page 69)

had the same father as my father, but not the same mother...Our barn had been attached to my grandfather's. When my father built the barn, Artshik was still a young boy. When grandpa and my father had already died, Artshik became the owner of two field shares. Since the barns were right next to each other, Artshik had the right [according to the Jewish religious concept] to appropriate our barn. And indeed, he took possession of it. When my mother said to him, "What's this about you taking a dvanoske [1] of rye from me?" he even began to strike. Out of meanness, he did other things to her as well...

When we came home for Sukkot, Mom told us how she suffers from our uncle Artshik. So we consulted that the best thing would be to look for a house and bring Mom to Bialystok with our little sister...

In the colony there was another family living in our house together with my mother. The man's name was *Meyer der Royter [Meyer the Red]* and his wife's name was *Leye Meyer's*. My mother rented them our house, sold the cattle and threshed out all the grain...

Meanwhile, my brothers and I rented a house in Bialystok with six rooms. We bought some furniture...We knew a man named *Dovid Itsi's.* He was a "leynketnik" [a foreman or master in the weaving mill]. He took out the warps [the threads stretched lengthwise in the loom] for weaving at Preyzman's. He built out a new house and rented it to us. His old house was in the yard, and his new house was in front, on the street. The street was called Yureftser Gas [Jurowiecka Street]. It was very close to the factory where I worked... When Mom and our little sister were already living with us, we were doing very well. Mom cooked for us and brought food to my brothers in the evening. We called this "vetshere" [dinner]. My little sister also brought me food twice a day...

We furnished our house very nicely. We were not doing badly, all of us earned money. Mom even rented another empty

_____

[1] a dvojniaczki, a utensil made of clay with two connected pots and a handle

(Page 70)

room in the house to two girls. They were sisters who were related to us by marriage, and they worked together with me. One was named *Sore*, the second *Tsivye*. *Rakhmiel*, my father's stepbrother [he and my father had a common father but not the same mother] married one of their sisters at that time. He was a handsome man, could write and teach. He taught me to write a letter within a month...

There is a lot to write about him. It was fashionable then for the young men who could write and teach to go to rich farmers in the villages to teach their children. My father's brother, Rakhmiel, was a teacher in the household at the parents of these two girls who had their quarters with us...Their parents maintained an estate called "Krole". It was not far from our colony, about four miles away, and to Bialystok it was also four miles. He [Rakhmiel] taught the boys and girls of the estate...The farmer was wealthy. My uncle Rakhmiel fell in love with his older daughter, whose name was Feygl. She was a tall, coarse, black, stuttering woman. He desired her because she had rich parents, a "gold mine"...But the gold melted away, only the pit remained. Their mother became ill and died...their father married for the second time and became impoverished... All the children had to flee...My uncle came to the colony with his wife Feygl and took possession of his piece of field, which he could claim from his brother Artshik...My uncle Rakhmiel already had two girls when he came to the colony. I forgot to write that the farmer's name was *Mendl Kroler*, and his wife's name was *Mindl*...Why am I writing down all this? Because it has to do with my uncle and my brother Alter. I will write about it later...

Well, my brothers and I didn't have any longer to stay in strange places and share a room with four of us, and now we already had six rooms. And my mother took care of the house very nicely...We were very happy. Guests used to come to me, to my brother Ishye and to the little children...

(Page 71)

40.

Let us now return to the young man I told you about before. My former landlady, with whom I lived on a street called "Unter der Turme" ["Behind the Prison"][1] or "Vashlikover Gas" [Wasilkowska Street], had determined at that time that the man should meet me in her daughter's garden during the day on Shabbat. However, she had not asked me beforehand, and I did not want to meet him[2]. The young man had come to the garden and was very angry, that I did not appear. He then told the landlady that he had another girl whom he loved. and with whom he had been in a relationship for a long time. Rokhel Itsi-Yankel's told me this shortly after...He, [the young man I describe,] came from the shtetl "Brok", near "Tshizever Oyezr" [Czyżew-Osada], "Lomzer gubernye" [Łomża Governorate], and not far from Lodzh...He had no parents left and had grown up with a rich uncle. And when he had that failure in the garden, he went to his uncle and told him everything. His uncle was a wise man and advised him to go back to Bialystok and to apologize. He followed his uncle, traveled to Bialystok, went to Rokhl Itsi-Yankel's and asked her to go to me together with him to ask for my forgiveness.

Together with Rokhel he went to my mother's house and asked her where I was. She answered that I was with my friend *Alte*, on Wasilkowska Street, not far from my former apartment.

---

[1] "Unter der Turme": Rachel sometimes uses the word "unter" [under] for "behind" in her regional dialect. In fact, the book "Zikhroynes un shriftn fun a Bialystoker" by Rachel's contemporary, Jacob Jerusalimski, indicates that the street was called "Hinter der Turme" ["Behind the Prison"] by other Jewish residents, see
Translation of the memoirs of Jakob Jerusalimski - Społeczne Muzeum Żydów Białegostoku i regionu (jewishbialystok.pl), page 11

[2] literally "her", but I think it's a typo.

As I was sitting and spending time with my friend Alte, the door opened and Rokhl came in to tell me that the young man she wanted to set me up with was standing outside and wanted to see me...I said to her, "oh what, is he going to tell me again that he has another girl?" Rokhl saw that I didn't want to see him, whereupon she asked my friend Alte to persuade me to go outside to see him. My friend Alte said to me, "go outside, he won't eat you up!"..

I went out to him and asked him what he wanted from me and why he had come. If it was just to tell me that he had another girl, he need not even bother. He said to me:

(Page 72)

"You know how it is when you're standing next to a cart, the cart goes off and you remain standing next to it like you're being pushed away, so I stayed in the garden..."

We started to go for a walk and had a good chat. When we came to our house, there were guests staying there. My cousin, *Libke,* had come to visit with her groom, also a young man from Odelsk named *Yoel.* He was in love with me. Earlier, when I came to the colony on holidays, he came to see me immediately, no matter whether it was thundering or lightning. But now that I no longer went to the colony, he had come to Bialystok to see me. He had come with other young people from the colony, and we had spent a nice time. Yoel was the son of *Henekh the Feldsher.* He himself was also a feldsher, and a feldsher in Odelsk was considered a doctor. There were no doctors in our country. He had a good reputation as a feldsher and earned very well. He was tall and handsome, and had a few freckles that suited him very well...He was elegant and dressed very nicely according to the latest fashion...He wanted me very much, but I didn't want him. I didn't suit any feldsher, but I liked to spend the time with him...

The young man I brought home was jealous of Yoel, and Yoel of him. They almost quarreled. In the end Yoel bade me farewell and went back to Odelsk. Since then I never saw him again. The young man I am telling about actually became my groom...When the company was gone, he felt relieved...It was cold in the house, we stood next to the wall of the small stove, warming ourselves and talking splendidly...

He did not own any good warm clothes. He was poor, had no warm coat, but wore just a scuffed cloak. But as soon as I fell in love with him, I didn't mind that he was poor and didn't earn much. He was a teacher, as I wrote earlier... I agreed to everything then because he was a handsome, athletic and also educated man. In fact, I fell in love with him and did not want to separate...

(Page 73)

My plan was that as soon as I earned six rubles a week as a warper, we would make a living...We got engaged. My groom was called *Avrom Itskhok*. He came to visit me every evening, since I worked during the day, and we were happy...

Later, however, great worries began. A teacher came in regularly to teach me Russian and some German. But my groom became jealous of this teacher and forbade him to come to me any more. The Russian teacher used to come twice a week before...And once, when the teacher told me that he would not any longer teach me, I asked him: "How come, why don't you want to teach me anymore? Am I not paying you?" He replied: "Your bridegroom has denied me to come to you any further. He said to me that his bride was already educated enough for him"...

41.

My groom, Avrom Itskhok, visited me very often, but not on Shabbat because he did not have nice garments. It seemed that he was very happy with the marriage. As a result of a foot disease, he could no longer go out to teach his lessons, earned nothing and had to starve quite a bit...He now wanted to get married and have a home as soon as possible. He knew I was earning and we would be able to make a living quite well on my earnings. For the time being, we would not rent a house; he lived in a room, so we would live in his room until we were financially settled. Finally, love don't put up a bill. For me everything was good, one could understand that. I didn't care what would happen later, only that I wanted to marry him. He was my great love. However, with him it was probably not like that...He had other thoughts. He would marry me and I would earn the money and give him a fine dowry of 300 rubles. It would be possible to do something with that...

His brother ran a "shpayz-krom", a grocery, as they say in America.

The store was on Nowolipie [Lipowa Street], the most beautiful

(Page 74)

street, and he made a good living...My groom figured that something could be done with my 300 rubles dowry and that one would certainly not go to the dogs... I, too, was confident that, like his brother, we would make a living. His brother's name was *Moyshe Mendl...*

But bad gossip began to make the rounds. The Russian teacher and my fiancé had become close friends. They used to meet on the street or somewhere else. Once my groom got angry and told the teacher that he would not marry me. He just wanted the dowry, the three hundred rubles, and then he was going to run away...

He [could have taken off with the dowry because he] was permitted to take out it. The money had been deposited with *Moyshe Brukh*, a very rich man and factory owner. He was the son-in-law of Arke Saraske, one of the powerful men and responsible people in Bialystok. My brother Ishye worked at Moyshe Brukh...When the teacher told the gossip to my brother Ishye, he went to my groom Avrom Itshkhok, insulted him and shook him like a herring so that he became afraid of my brother...My brother Ishye was a very strong man...My groom said that this was a big lie. He had never said this, he had never wanted the wedding to go off...

I was not aware of it, and when my mother told me about it, I quarreled so violently with my brother Ishye that my brother wanted to move out of our house. We didn't speak to each other for the long time until the wedding...I was sick and devastated, didn't want to speak to anyone, but only cried because of my great misfortune...

My groom was also sick with anger. He might have said that in jest, but those kinds of jokes were now becoming great sorrow for both of us...

42.

Once my groom dined in the "gorkikh" [restaurant] not far from where he lived, where a girl I knew worked. He asked the girl to go and visit me. He wrote a few

(Page 75)

words that he was not feeling well and I had to come visit him...My mother, may she rest in peace, went to see him and he passed on to her the request that I should come to him, that he would explain everything to me and that I would understand him. This was on a Shabbat, he was sick and was unable to come to see me...

My mother assured him that I would come to see him. And so it happened...I went to see him immediately, and he was indeed sick. His feet were not healthy. They had fallen ill when he was serving the Tsar...Every soldier had to serve four years at that time. But he, my groom, had to serve five years because he had escaped from military service. When he was caught, he was put in the prison, that is, in a dark, cold room, where he fell ill on his feet...

When I visited him that Shabbat, he was very happy and told me that he had been very sick all week and could not get up. Whenever he felt a little better, he went to the "gorkikh".

We became a couple again and he asked that my mother come to him and discuss with him when the wedding would take place...He asked me to go through another street because in Bialystok it did not make a good impression when the bride goes to the groom's house...He wanted to protect me from being talked badly about...

Oh, what a room it was in which he lived! It was dark, without a window, and what a bed it was! The bed was propped up from below with pieces of wood. There was no chair to sit on. So I sat down on the bed, which almost toppled over. And what scraps were lying around in the small room! The landlord couple was poor, the husband made a living by mending old things, and there were old rags that he mended thrown all over the house...

When I left the house, the landlady was running after me, telling me that he [my groom] had become sick with grief because it hurt him that the wedding had fallen through. And now he was in seventh heaven with joy that we had reconciled.

(Page 76)

And love demands no reckoning. I loved him so much that it didn't impress me that he was poor and sick. On the contrary, I loved him even more dearly...

43.

My mother visited my bridegroom and made arrangements with him for the wedding to take place a week before Passover. There was rejoicing and joy, and preparations were already being made for the wedding. A "garnitur" was bought [1] for him, in our country it is called a "suit", and a long tailcoat with a long slit from the bottom.

They bought for him a warm coat, shoes, and also a high top hat, as was the fashion, and a few nice shirts.

Thursday was already to be the wedding, and I remember how he came a day early and asked for something. I mean he wanted the things I already listed. If he didn't get them, he wouldn't go to the wedding, and besides, he wanted fifty rubles...There were already challah, gingerbread and bread baked...Poultry, meat and fish were already provided, and everything was prepared for a beautiful wedding...He ran away angrily. Everyone was very frightened and the groom was no longer trusted...

Together with the cook, my mother went to see him. He lived on "Khanaykes"[Chanajki], this was the poorest area [2]. On Chanaiki lived the chimney sweeps and those who cleaned the privies. They were considered to be the humblest people. The underworld also lived on Chanajki. On Shabbat, boys and girls used to gather to learn to dance... "Izvoshtshikes" (coachmen) and alley boys used to gather here, and on Shabbat they used to prepare for carousals. The street had the worst reputation...

---

[1] I think that she means "ordered"

[2] Anyone who wants to know more about the Bialystok quarter "khanaykes"[Chanajki] will find a loving, detailed account in Jacob Jerusalimski's biography. Jacob grew up in this quarter and was a contemporary of Rachel, see Translation of the memoirs of Jakob Jerusalimski - Społeczne Muzeum Żydów Białegostoku i regionu (jewishbialystok.pl), page 14

I come back to my groom, Avrom Itskhok. I already mentioned that Mom went to him with the cook. He said that if they gave him the fifty rubles and bought for him the things he asked for, the wedding would take place. In fact, they didn't trust him anymore, but they were ashamed to let the wedding go off. And I

(Page 77)

still had a crush on him... Well, my mother, oleyo hasholem [may she rest in peace], let him have the fifty rubles. He went to a men's clothing store and picked out the things I listed earlier. The owner of the store brought the things to our home and we paid for them...

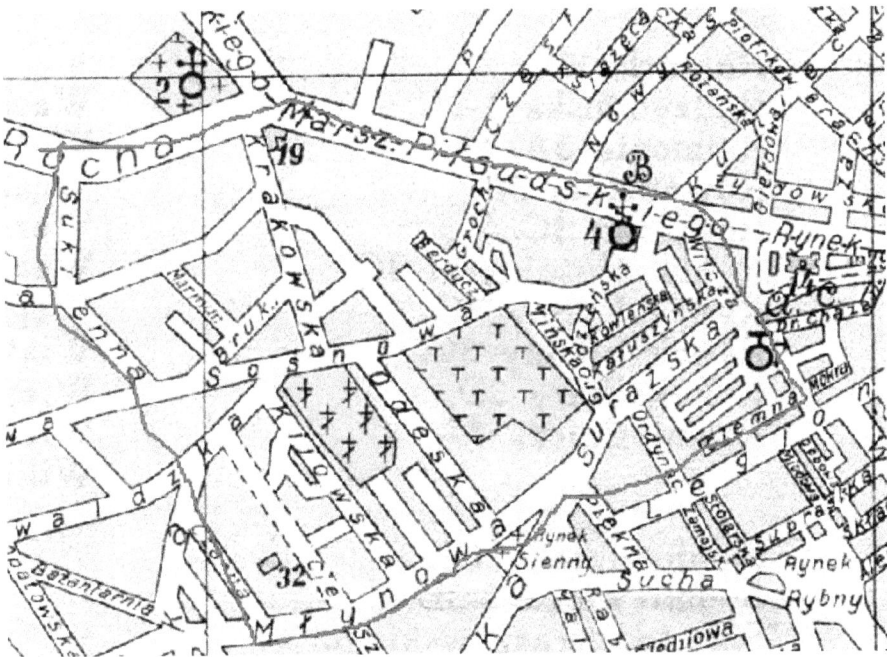

Excerpt of a Bialystoker map from 1935 (with the area of Khanaykes/Chanajki in its center, the red line is made by me), courtesy of Dr.Tomek Wisniewski

My brother Ishye was 18 years old at that time and my brother Note was 15. I remember how worried my brothers were at that time, they were so young, but they saw more than I saw at that time...

1161. Bialystock - Im alten Stadtteil Kainiki.

Old card of Khanaykes/Chanajki/Kainiki, courtesy of Dr. Tomek Wisniewsk

i

The old Bialystok prison today, photo courtesy of Dr. Tomek Wisniewski

The old prison in Bialystok, photo courtesy of Dr.Tomek Wisniewski

Bialystok, Lipowa Street, photo courtesy of Dr.Tomek Wisniewski

Suraska Sreet in Bialystok, old photograph courtesy of Dr. Tomek Wisniewski

БѢЛОСТОКЪ. – BIALYSTOK. – BIALYSTOK.
Тыкоцкая (Лип.) удиц. – Tykozkastrasse
Ulica Tykozka.

Bialystok, old card, courtesy of Tomek Wisniewski

44.

The wedding took place on Thursday in 1895, and it was a very beautiful wedding...At the factory where I had worked for many years, everyone was good friends with me, and they all came to my wedding. The master, his name was *Shmulek*, a young and handsome man, the weavers and all my comrades were at the wedding. Together, all of them from the factory had bought me a beautiful wedding present: A samovar with a beautiful tray and glasses. Preyzman's factory was on Jurowiecka Street, where we also lived, and where the wedding took place. Not far from our house there was a hall on Jurowiecka Street.

I had dressed up in a beautiful white wedding dress, a "galandre"[1] and white shoes-all in white, as befits a bride. I had bought green plush from my manufacturer and had a cape sewn, a long tippet that reached down to my shoes. It was like a coat, only without sleeves. On top of the long tippet was another short tippet...It had cost a lot of money. The plush had cost five rubles per cubit, and sewing it cost about twenty rubles. The lining fabric was good satin.

---

[1] a decorative accessory, in this case I think that a veil is meant.

The plush I had bought on installments...The things for my wedding cost a few hundred rubles...These were taken over by my mother and my brothers. My brothers worked and gave their earnings to my mother. Mom was responsible for the budget expenses and saved for the wedding...I also earned and saved for the wedding 300 rubles dowry.

(Page 78)

When my mother was still in the colony, I could not even save a ruble. I had to support my brothers, because they earned nothing. Besides, I sent my mother as much as I could. After that, when my brothers also earned money I could save for my dowry. Without a dowry one could not marry. But when I had the three hundred rubles, I could choose the groom I loved. And I really loved Avrom Itskhok more than anything. I felt as if I could not live without him...However, when we were already all in the hall, with all the musicians, with everyone who attended the wedding, and it was getting late, my groom still had not appeared. So people were still worried that he was already regretting the wedding. But when he finally came, joy came again...

The guests were all from our family, as his family did not show up because it was close to Passover and it was too far for them to come to us. His uncles and cousins lived in the small town of Brok, which is next to Tshizeve [Czyżew-Osada], on the route to Warsaw. Only his sister *Sheyne Khaye* had come from Tshizeve, and all alone, because her husband was in America. She came with a big wig over her forehead, and I also had to wear a wig. He wanted to boast about marrying a pious woman...

45.

Now I'll tell you about the time after the wedding. We didn't stock up on furniture like we did there in America. Over Shabbat we stayed with Mom and my brothers. My mother had a beautiful home with six rooms. But my husband didn't want to live with them...You had to perform the "sheve-brokhes" [the gathering of the guests in the house of the newlyweds on Friday night after the wedding]. It was a ritual in Russia among both poor and rich people to have "sheve-brokhes" on Shabbat and, also on Shabbat, to take the bride and groom to the synagogue...I remember how women, my acquaintances, came and led me to the synagogue...The

(Page 79)

synagogue was in Jurowiecka Street, not far from our house. It was a rich synagogue. Madam Preyzman also prayed in that synagogue. She came to me and congratulated me, and my mother and I invited her for gingerbread and liquor. She didn't shy away coming to our house, and that was really a great honor that such a rich madam like *Hinde Preyzman* goes to her worker for gingerbread and schnapps.

Madam Preyzman was fat and not tall, but she was very smart. She was involved in the factory's affairs, and every day she and her husband went around the factory to see how the work was going...

And since I'm already talking about the factory, let me describe it a little bit more. The factory was not only a weaving mill, but it also had "a parovke oyf pare", a steam mill, how they call it in America, and a dye house and related machinery to prepare the wool for dyeing. There were all kinds of machines all over the house. One brought the wool from the sheep and processed it there until the cloth was ready for sale...

In the "kantor" (office) worked accountants who were members of [the owner's] family. I remember that one accountant was the brother of Madam Preyzman. His name was *Belakh* and he lived on Gumyaner Gas [Gumienna Street]. The street led into Jurowiecka Street. Another accountant was the older son-in-law, who also held a small share in the partnership...

Mr. Preyzman was a tall and handsome man and could study many disciplines. He was pious, and when I went to work in the morning, I saw him praying in the Bes-Medresh...Madam Preyzman was also pious and wore her wig pulled down to her forehead. The Preyzman's had four daughters and two sons. Only one, the oldest, was already married. She was not really beautiful, was very fat and could hardly lift her feet. This is not an exaggeration, it is true what I write. I used to visit the eldest daughter. She lived on the second floor in her parents' house. When she became ill, she did not want to see any other girl except me. She took pleasure in talking to me and when they called me to the house, I had to go to her. I did not like this, but I did not know how to help myself.

(Page 80)

Her husband was handsome and learned. I have not checked this to be sure, but so they said in the town...

The Preyzman's used to look for spouses for their children abroad or in deep Russia...

46.

Now I will describe Preyzman's house where they lived and the other buildings on their yard [1]. They lived in a wooden house with two floors. There were eight rooms downstairs and four upstairs. They were millionaires and lived in a wooden house...I don't want to say that it was not beautiful inside the house. There was the most beautiful furniture there and a very classy piano that the girls played on.

In front of their house was the office, and behind the house on the side was another small house where I with another girl prepared warp yarn tapes...and here the weavers took over the warps to weave...

Behind the small cottage was di "parovke" [steam mill] with the large chimneys. The "parovke" was a building with three floors. In this building the wool was prepared, which came in sacks from the sheep to the weaver... No, of course it came before to the spinners, and after the spinning to the bobbin winders and the warpers, and from the warpers finally to the weavers...After that they took the material and sent it to another place, which was called "poletur "place. And from here, the finished pieces of cloth left.

---

[1] Their house was located on the factory premises.

On the other side of the large factory was another building with two floors. Here was the weaving mill. Sixty weavers worked there...and you can imagine what a hustle and bustle there was...Six o'clock in the morning the steams whistled, and at eight o'clock again, because the workers were to have breakfast. Then again at 12 o'clock because the workers were to have lunch. And in the evening, when the workers were supposed to go home, the steam whistled again...Why am I describing this? Because the Preyzman's were so rich and powerful, but lived in a wooden house...Imagine if here in America such a millionaire lived right next to his factories?!

(Page 81)

And in such a way that every morning at six o'clock there was a great deal of commotion, and it hummed and roared all day long, and they [the Preyzman's] have always lived there...

I worked for them until my wedding, for eight years, and also after the wedding, until I had my first child. They were the best factory owners in Bialystok. Jewish weavers, old people with their sons and sons-in-law worked for them for years.

Why am I describing them in such detail? Because Mrs. Preyzman was so good to me on the Shabbat when I was led to the synagogue, and she came to our house for gingerbread and schnapps after the prayer...She knew my husband and his brother, because he had married her maid. She knew that my husband was a teacher, and the "shidekh" [marital union] pleased her very much...I must write more about them later.

After my marriage, my husband did not want to live with my family and I had to go to his small room, "untern oyvn" [behind the stove]. But I loved him so much that everything was fine and dandy for me, even going "untern oyvn" with him. There was no window there, yet it was dear to me...

47.

After Passover, right after our wedding, I already had to go back to my work because my husband was very sick in his feet after all and could not go to his lessons. Early in the morning, when I got up, I prepared a vessel of warm water for him, soaked his feet in it, smeared them with ointment and wrapped them in bandages. I prepared breakfast for him and went to the factory...

For two weeks he was bedridden. After that he got better and left home to find employment, teaching children on an hourly basis. When he became ill, he lost his employments...I remember that when he started teaching after Passover, he earned 19 rubles a month. A week before Shvues [Shavuot], however, it was only 10 rubles a month. When I saw that he earned so little, I gave him my rubles every week that I earned, and he kept the household's budget.

(Page 82)

He was very good to me. Every day he accompanied me to work and picked me up from there. It was a very long way from the factory on Jurowiecka Street to [Chanajki, where we lived...

It went on like that for five months. After the five months, my husband went to withdraw some money from the dowry. He bought beds and other furniture from it, and rented an apartment not far from the factory, actually on Jurowiecka Street, next to Bialystotsek [Bialystoczek]. It was a very nice apartment. It was located at our acquaintance's house, where I used to shop before I got married. Our acquaintance was a baker, he owned a stone house with a big bakery and an apartment for himself. And what an apartment it was! He lived with his family like millionaires. They had a big store next to the town clock, where they sold bread, challah and all kinds of pastries...

But man proposes, God disposes. Something happened to the baker, but I don't know what; a "secret" surrounded him, a condemnation, and he was sent to Siberia. His wife went after him, smuggled him out in the middle of the way, and the two of them fled to America...When I came to America ten years later, I met them in New York on Essex Street. They ran a big bakery on Essex Street. I also lived on Essex Street and bought bread, challah and cakes from them, which were just as tasty as in Bialystok...They were very good to us when we lived with them in Bialystok. And when I came to America and met such good friends again, I promptly bought everything from them again. I was also very pious in America and carried the "tsholent" stew for Shabbat to them so that they would put it in their oven...It was to this baker that I moved, this was my first apartment in Bialystok after the wedding. In that apartment I also bore my eldest daughter, *Mine*...

My husband was very happy to have such a beautiful apartment. It was a garret. We had two beautiful polished beds that looked like they were made of mahogany. I had two beautiful "kapes" for them, here they call it "bedspreads". I laid out the beds like sofas. Everything was very nice in the room...

(Page 83)

48.

When the summer had passed and the holidays were approaching, my Avrom Itskhok told me that he was going to Brok to visit his family. In Brok my husband had his whole family, uncles and cousins. There was one uncle he liked especially, his name was *Sokher* and he was really a beautiful person and also a rich merchant. He used to trade with wood, together with his son, *Shloyme*. Uncle Sokher had no wife and lived with his son and his family, a wife and four children. It was a very nice house with about ten rooms. One room was very large, about 50 feet in length and 50 feet in width [15.24m x 15.24 m]...He [my husband] had another uncle whom he did not like. He was divorced and they called him *"the Gorush"* [the divorced one]...He was rich and gave interest-bearing loans. However, he was stingy and always wore the same coat. He was actually handsome, tall, and no fool. He also came to see me...My husband had a [half] sister with a different mother from him. She invited us to a guest dinner...A second son of Uncle Sokher, who was older than Shloyme, lived a little further. We visited him too and had a banquet...Uncle Sokher had another daughter, *Khaye*, who was blind in one eye. Her husband's name was Isroel. He was very handsome and could study. Uncle Sokher was rich, so he was able to marry off his half-blind daughter to a handsome fellow. She also invited us to a guest dinner...

What a joy I had on that Sukes [Sukkot] when I went with my husband to his shtetele Brok; this is 59 years ago now. My husband's family said to my Avrom Itskhok that he should give me a pleasure and go rowing with me on the "Nyeman" [Neman]...It was on the 7th day of Sukkot. The Neman, a very big river, flowed about half a block away behind the uncle's house. My husband took a boat that you move with oars, and we rowed for a few hours. And my husband knew how to row! His uncle Sokher owned quite a few "lodkes" (boats.)

(Page 84)

I am just thinking that I was the luckiest person in the world at that time. My beloved husband gave me so much happiness...That was so many years ago now, and now that I am writing it down, my husband has been dead for 26 years...As I write, it seems like it was just then...yet so many years have passed, and I was so happy then. I can't even put it into words. My husband was an educated and handsome man, just as I had wished. Before I got married, I wished that even if I had to go to work after the wedding, I would still want to have a man who was handsome, smart and educated. And indeed, such a man met me...Although there were misunderstandings before the wedding and I would be afraid that worries would arise...But when my husband had shown me so much love on that Sukkot and his family had welcomed me so finely, he was the very dearest in the world to me...

49.

When we came back to Bialystok, I was already pregnant. My husband took the matter seriously. If our child was born, I would not be able to go to work, and there were only 150 rubles left of the dowry. So he was looking for something to trade. My husband's brother, Moyshe Mendl, had a store on Nowolipie [Lipowa Street] which secured his income. In addition, he was a "protsentnik" [usurer]; he was considered a rich man. He was indeed rich. My husband found a "store" directly across the street from his brother. But it was not a real store, it was a pavilion, like a candy store here in America. This was all shortly after we returned from the shtetl Brok where we "were on a visit". In America this is called a "honeymoon". We had as much fun as on a "honeymoon".

So, we came back to Bialystok and all the pleasures were already over. Serious facts now had to be created. My husband bought the pavilion opposite his brother's store. It was already winter, and in winter you cannot make any profit from a pavilion. So

(Page 85)

my husband sat in the pavilion all day long and froze, but the income was barely enough for the apartment rent...

[At the beginning of the] summer we could make a lot of money in the pavilion, and it was enough for living. So we hoped to have enough to live on all summer. After Shavuot I had to give up my job, and at the beginning of the month of Tamez (June-July) I was to give birth. I gave up the position in the factory and went to help my husband in the pavilion...

Fortunately, another business opportunity arose. Not far from the town there was a "yevonim" [regiment of soldiers] and it was necessary to supply them with food, i.e. provisions. My husband's brother found out about it and hired my husband as a partner. My husband's brother could neither write nor speak Russian, unlike my husband, Avrom Itskhok. My husband's brother, *Moyshe Mendl*, also could not keep books and accounts, so my husband took care of the books. Moyshe Mendl provided the money to supply the soldiers with provisions.

I had already given birth [1] and could not be in the pavilion. But my little sister came and stood in the pavilion for a short time until I would have regained my strength. My sister was nine years old then, but already a mature girl...

The soldiers did not stay longer than three months and then returned to Warsaw. Together with my husband and our daughter Mushe (who was named after his mother, whom he loved very much), I lived on Jurowiecka Street. The store, i.e. the pavilion, and thus also our "salon" [in the sense of our center of life], were located far from our apartment. I could not drag myself so far with the child...But there was a chamber next to the "salon" that could be rented. If we lived close enough to the "salon", I would be able to help my husband...The chamber was too small, but since I had to help my husband, we had no other choice. We gave up the beautiful apartment and moved into the chamber.

But here the problems began. The landlady of the chamber where we now lived was a Jewish woman with two daughters. One daughter had just returned from America, where she had completed an apprenticeship as a beautician.

---

[1] we will hear about her first baby, Mushe, later.

(Page 86)

She opened a "beauty-parlor" in Bialystok, that is, a salon where one could have oneself made beautiful, and earned a lot of money. She had a sister whom she also taught this craft. Unfortunately, her sister had a hunchback. She was a very fine and good person. The older one, however, was not a bad one either...The two sisters made a lot of money. The older sister was called by the rich women to their homes to beautify "their heads". She could also make wigs, she had learned that even before she had gone to America...They lived in a beautiful house on Nowolipie [Lipowa Street]. We had rented a chamber from them and were also allowed to use the kitchen...However, I became very jealous of the older sister because she spent so much time with my husband in the pavilion. It made me so nervous that I approached him about why she was always in the "store" when I came to help him...My husband told her about it, and she replied that she was sitting in the store having a pastry, a glass of water, halvah [dessert], or other snack. I believed her. However, I suspected her; now I think I was just jealous, and that's all.

50.

My sister usually came in and looked after my little daughter. Sometimes my mother, oleyo hasholem, [may she rest in peace], also came in, and so my husband could take care of his "podryat" [sub-contract work] of delivering provisions. Every day he had to go to buy products for the soldiers...In the pavilion it had already become more lively. I took care of it, and it already looked nicer inside, so you could also go inside the pavilion and spend a little more money...

A quarrel started between my husband and my mother... When I was still living on Jurowiecka Street and our child was two months old, my mother used to come to our apartment to help me and bring lunch to my husband. My husband allotted me household money for each day, and when my mother saw that it was not enough, she approached my husband about it. Thus, hatred arose between him and

(Page 87)

my mother, almost throughout her life. He became my mother's enemy for no reason. He didn't know that with a small child you needed more money...

Before this dispute had developed, on the first Yom Kippur with him before I had my child, he had taken me to my mother and brothers to wish them a good year. I remember being the happiest in the world at that time. We were still living in his room behind the stove, but those times were the best for us. I thought then that it would always be that good. But things don't turn out the way man thinks. Man proposes, God disposes...[1]

The summer was coming to an end, and we took in very little at the pavilion. My husband had saved up quite a few rubles from the income of the "podryat" with his brother and he planned to go to London, learn a job there, and take me and our child to London a little later...And if everything worked out well and we had a little money saved up, we would go to America. But it didn't turn out the way he thought it would. He couldn't find work in London, and he didn't bring any manual skills from home either. He left the pavilion to me. My mother looked after our child, and when she had to go to make food for my brothers and do the housework, my little sister came to look after my child...

Thus passed a whole winter. Young people left debts to us after taking snacks with us, and I reminded them. I had enough income for the winter and the beginning of summer...I got a letter from my husband that he was thinking of coming home. He was longing for me and the child and had not earned any income...

I myself with my child also had nothing left for living, and not even money for the apartment rent. Therefore, my mother and my brothers took me in. It was a bit cramped, but what else could they do with me and a small child...They lived in an attic apartment with two rooms...

I cannot describe the longing I had for my husband. He wrote to me that he was struggling a lot and didn't know what to do.

---

[1] literally: "der mentsh trakht un got lakht", "man plans and God laughs".

He wanted to come home, but had no money for a ship ticket. So I went to his brother, Moyshe Mendl, and asked him to send him the money as an advance. But the latter did not want to know anything about it. He answered me that Avrom Itskhok had not asked him whether he should go to London, and now he did not want to know anything about him. He was a rich man, but no faithful brother. He also told me that this was the reason he did not go to his brother's wedding, because he had already guessed that he would not provide a living and that I would eventually come to him for money. This was the end. I wished him a good day and off I went.

When I got home and told my brothers, they immediately sent 50 rubles to him the next day. He had only asked for forty rubles, but my brothers thought that they should send him ten rubles more so that he would not have to skimp because of a few rubles and would have enough for the trip.

51.

My two brothers, Note and Alter, were still very young. The older brother, Ishye, was already married. He had married soon after my little daughter, Mushe, was born, and I could not go to his wedding. My child was only two months old. His wedding took place in Krynki, which was six miles from Bialystok. However, my husband, Avrom Itskhok, did go to this wedding...

My younger brothers had to go to work and take care of my mother with my sister, Sheyne Gitl, and me and my child. And they were so kind-hearted and also went to borrow money to send to my husband to come home...I remember when he came home, I asked my brother, Alter, to ask for a job at his workplace, if maybe I could prepare the warp yarn tapes there. However, to be assigned enough work as a warper, you have to work in a large factory, and my brother Alter worked in a small factory. He actually got a small job for me as a warper, but it wasn't enough for living expenses...Many good friends were looking for jobs for me because they knew I was a good warper.

Krynki, photo courtesy of Dr. Tomek Wisniewski

Krynki, photo courtesy of Dr. Tomek Wisniewski

(Page 89)

They began to call me to three small factories where they assigned me work. My mother, brothers and little sister rented an apartment in another street nearby, and gave us their previous apartment. It was a nice apartment, the windows faced the street, and the street was very nice.

I had already settled in at home. We had two beds, which we had bought when I moved to Jurowiecka Street, and which in the meantime stood at my mother's...Now, when my mother moved with the children to the other apartment, the beds remained and we made do with what we had.

I remember how happy we were when my husband came back from London. He found me with my mother and brothers. *Mushele*, who had been named after his mother, may she rest in peace, was as beautiful as the sun. I hoped that with time I would get more work, he would also find a job and we would already get along...

52.

One Shabbat afternoon my husband invited me for a walk. We went in "Unter der Turme" ["Behind the Prison"], a wide path on which one went to Vashilikove [Vashlikov]. Now listen to what he told me: He said that as it looked, he would not be able to make a living. Therefore, he wanted me to do something to stop having children...I answered him that I did not want such a life. I would never do anything that would make my body sick, and I wanted to have children. If he, my husband, did not want to have children, we could divorce... In response, he said: "You can see that I can't make a living. What will be then? The children will only toil"...I answered him that we will see later. I would like to have children and I wanted to have children. And I really carried this out!

It was not long before I became pregnant again...My second child was born with a caul, on Friday night, in 1898...I had worked all Friday at the factory, had been preparing the warp yarn tapes, and when I came home in the evening, I said the Blessing of the Light and prepared for dinner. My mother had cooked for the whole family.

(Page 90)

She had cooked noodles with beans and I ate my fill; there were also other dishes. After two hours had passed, I called my mother to send for the "bobe" [grandma], (the Jewish woman who took the children from their mothers was called the "bobe"). When the "bobe" arrived, the child was already born and they were just waiting for her to cut the umbilical cord...

Everyone was happy that I had been working hard all day, had already given birth at ten o'clock in the evening and was feeling quite well. There was no better cause for joy...

You're not supposed to light a fire on Shabbat. So my brother, Alter, took the tiny child to the window, through which there was a glow of light. And when he saw how the little baby shone, he shouted that it was an angel, because it shone like the sun and the moon. And he was really holding the child against the glow of the moon at the window...You can imagine how a woman feels who has just delivered a child, lifting her head and seeing her brother holding the little swaddled creature in his arms and playing with him in the glow of the moon...Do you think he was mistaken? No. The girl was a beauty! We called her Libe, after my father, may he rest in peace. As you know, my father's name was Leybe...

And my Libele grew into a beauty and was so well turned out...She learned very well and is actually a physician, and I have much joy with her, and she is very good to me. She supports me a lot in life and when I am in need, she gives me a lot of money. She understands what I lack and I never regretted that I wanted to have children...

But now I'm too far ahead. I shouldn't have written this yet...I'm going back now to when my husband came back from London and didn't have a job. I was pregnant and working in two or three factories...And since in all three factories the warp yarn tapes had to be prepared, guess what I did? I first prepared the warp yarn tapes in one factory, later in the second

(Page 91)

factory, and in the evening until twelve o'clock in the third factory. And there, where I worked at night, the weaver used to sit with me and walk me home because that was when I was already heavily pregnant...

I forgot to write that when I gave birth to Libele, my husband was not at home. He was in a different city. Also, I forgot to write that when I gave birth to Libele on Friday night, there was only a small kerosene lamp burning. It was dark, and therefore my brother took the newborn to the window, in the glow of the moon...With my first child, Mushele, I had a very difficult birth. I was in labor all day, and they hung me from a rope on the ceiling. A doctor was present, and my husband was called to be present at the birth, because it was considered a charm.

53.

I had a cousin, he was the son of my father's brother. My uncle was called *Motl Shmuel*, and my cousin was called *Leyzer Meyer*. Leyzer Meyer was already married, but also already divorced. He stayed with his rich sister on Nowolipie [Lipowa Street]. He had no place to go in and to pour out his broken heart to anyone. So he came to me when he had time. And when he saw me struggling with the two tiny children who were so beautiful (I am not exaggerating, the two girls were rare beauties), my cousin said to me:

"Listen, Rokhl-Anna, I will do you a favor. When I go to America, I will give my job to your husband!" You had to be an educated man to do that, and my husband really was an educated man. It was a job as a sales representative for the Singer sewing machine company. He had to find customers who wanted to buy the sewing machines. He used to drive around looking for customers. And this was the reason that my husband was not at home when I gave birth to Libele. When he came back, he was very happy that the child was so beautiful and healthy and my birth so easy.

My husband invited his "farvalter", (that is, his manager)

(Page 92)

to eat with us when he would be in our area...And when the manager actually came and no one was home to clean up the apartment, I got up from the crib, mopped the floor and got sick. Twenty-two weeks I was sick. Twice a week, my husband took me to a good doctor, until I got well again...

Before I got Libele, I taught my little sister the craft of warping...my sister was so young, no older than twelve, but she was already working diligently. She prepared all the warp yarn tapes and we shared the work and the earnings. But, I had to have someone to take care of the children, so I had to look for someone. I could not pay for a normal nanny. So I hired an old gentile, however, she neglected my children![1] I can't tell you how sick I felt. My mother was no longer in Bialystok, she could not stand the weather there in the city and was sick all the time. As a result, the doctors told her to go back to the colony. My brothers gave her money so that she could buy a cow. And the piece of field she still owned was enough for her to make a living. Alter, Note and my little sister rented a room and my sister cooked for them...

When my brother Alter turned twenty-one and had to report for military service, but did not want to serve for "fonye" [the Tsar], he inflicted damage on himself. However, it did not help, he was enlisted as a soldier. He escaped from military service and went to America, and it was a miracle of God that he was not caught. However, he remained sick all his life...

54.

And now I come back to myself and my problems...My mother was already back in the colony, getting healthier and living in her own house, which she had not sold at that time. She had rented it to our acquaintance, whose name was *Meyer*

(Page 93)

Leyzer's. His father's name was *Leyzer the Red*, and his [son's] wife was *Leye Meyer's...* When my mother came to the colony and couldn't get an apartment, Meyer Leyzer's provided her with a chamber... That was even better for Mom, because she didn't have to be alone in the house, but lived with other people.

---

[1] "hot zi mir farlozn bay di kindern di kep": It is likely that she neglected especially the hygiene of the head and hair area of the kids.

Once she came to visit us in Bialystok. She had to say goodbye to Note, who was also preparing to leave for America...She came to my house, of course. It was only a short period of time until my brother Notke would leave. I still remember the quarrel that my husband used to raise with my mother. Always arguing and chasing after my mother and my little sister...What do you think I said to him? I told him, "if you are going to hurt my mother and my sister, I will take a pot of hot water and scald you"...

Well, imagine that, he already earned a few rubles and I say to him that I will scald him with a pot of water. He started shouting, and at his shouting my brother Notke came running, grabbed him by the hand and said, "I can shake you like straw!" He [my husband] was ashamed and went away...

For two weeks he did not come home...I went to the "kantor" (office) of "Singer sewing machines" and told them that my husband had not come home for two weeks already. They replied that they had sent him to another city to take orders for Singer sewing machines. At the office, the people were very kind to me and asked me if I needed money. But I said that I didn't need money and I just didn't know what to make of the fact that my husband hadn't come home for two weeks. They told me that they would send him home as soon as he came to the office. They understood that we had been arguing...

When he came into the office, they told him that they could tell from my face how worried I had been. They asked if something had happened between us? Well, he ran home quickly, even before he had handed in the list of orders he had made on the way...When he got home, he acted as if nothing was wrong. No one from my family was at home anymore; my mother had already gone back to the colony. My brother Notke

(Page 94)

had left for America. My sister Sheyne Gitl had gotten a very nice room in the home of a mother with three daughters. The girls were also warpers that their mother had trained. She usually cooked food for her children and now she was cooking for my sister as well...My sister lived with them until she went to America...

Now I'm coming back to me and my husband. Life became so bitter that I can't describe it...Just when we both wanted to forget our quarrels, they freshened up each time...I harbored so much resentment toward him for being so bad to my mother and sister...I used to nurse my little daughter and then go to my sister's factory to bring her lunch. In the evening I brought [my sister] dinner...Friday I let her have a [festive] Shabbat meal; I made sure that my sister did not feel miserable. Since she didn't want to come to me, I carried my children to her every Shabbat...

It was already becoming a bit more relaxed at home. However, I told you that the old gentile [neglected] my children, so they got cold, and my beautiful girls developed scrofula. The younger daughter tore off her skin. The old gentile also didn't want to be with me anymore, it was too hard for her. She left me. I therefore said to my husband that he must take care of the children while I am at work, because after all he does not work. So he looked after the children, but when he went away to town, he left the children with our neighbor. He was a cobbler and worked at home. We lived on the second floor, and the cobbler was directly across. My husband became good friends with the cobbler and his wife, but the cobbler had to work. He couldn't spend time with our children, and neither could his wife. When I came home and found my children in a bad condition, I cried. He [my husband] resented me for this. There was another quarrel between us, and my husband disappeared again...

We stayed with a landlady. She came from the shtetl Yaneve [Janow Podlaski], from where they sent her a young girl, an orphan. She was 13 years old. My landlady saw

(Page 95)

the problems I was facing: I had to go to work, but I had no one to leave the children with, and so I was in danger of losing my job at the factory and with it my whole livelihood. She let the girl work with me, her name was *Kroyne*...My landlady also brought back my husband. She had seen him somewhere on the street and asked him to come home and have a talk with me. In fact, he came right away...

55.

The girl from Yaneve was still a child, but she nursed my children very well. She even cooked for us. The children were violently afflicted with scrofula and she had to take care of them...she had a hard job and she didn't stay with us for long...

The landlady moved to America. Her husband was already there, near San Francisco, where they were digging for gold. Anyway, her husband had come back to Bialystok for a few months, bought a few houses and then went back to America. I lived in one of those houses. Now, when his wife also wanted to go to America, she sold the houses. In America, she learned that my cousin, *Yisroel Khayim*, was her sister's husband...

When Kroyne left me, I cried and lamented. What was I supposed to do now? I had to go to work! My husband could not stay with the children all the time, he had to go back to work and sell Singer sewing machines. So we had to take the old gentile back. She was already 75 years old and you even still had to take care of her...such an old woman, but we could not afford a good maid. So I gave my sister my job in two small factories, and kept only one. This allowed me to take care of the children a little more...

The children had already grown up, but there was no peace in our house. There was already something torn between us, and all the mending was useless. Our life was also torn apart, and since we could not repair it, everything just fell apart. My great love for him

(Page 96)

turned into bitterness and darkness, and we no longer had any respect for each other. But since we were responsible for the children, it dragged on like that...

News was making the rounds. When war broke out between Japan and Russia, my husband was still a conscript soldier. He was very much in fear and was preparing to leave for America...He asked his company for some money from his customers' deposits for the Singer sewing machines, but received barely enough money for his expenses...His superiors could not know what he was up to because he always went away for a few weeks anyway to take orders and claim money. He left me his accounts and the papers. But I was not to hand them in until he was already in America. However, his superiors learned that my husband had gone to America and came to me to demand the accounts and papers. I told them to come a few weeks later and they would get the accounts and papers...

Fayvl and Rivke Rokhel lived on Nowolipie [Lipowa Street] where they had a large men's goods store. Why do you think I carried the papers and accounts to Fayvl and Rivke Rokhl? Rivke Rokhl was my cousin from the same colony. She was the daughter of my uncle *Motl Shmuel*. Therefore, I trusted them with the papers and the accounts...

When my husband left for America, my older daughter was 5 1/2 years old and the younger one was 3 years old. I stayed alone with the small children. All of my family were already in America, only my mother was still in Russia. She was in Krynki and had married for the second time. So I stayed alone with my two sick children and had nothing to live on...

My feeling had predicted that I would have problems with my husband. And so it was. When he arrived in America he wrote a letter denouncing my brothers and my sister. My sister was still angry with him at that time. I wrote to him that he himself had been very bad to my sister and my mother, which is why my sister did not pick him up when he arrived by ship...My brother Ishye Velvel lived

(Page 97)

in Hoboken and was also angry with my husband for gossiping...My sister, Sheyne Gitl, lived in Paterson, and my brother Notke, who was still a young lad, lived with Alter.

And my brother Notke was a good-natured person. He picked up my husband from the ship and brought him home to Alter. He also helped him out with a few dollars...

56.

My husband learned to sew children's pants in New York, however, he could not make much for me and the kids. He relied on my brother, Notke. But Notke could not fully support me either. I had to try again to get work as a warper...But how could I do that with two small children? I couldn't even go and look for work, because I had to take the children with me. And no one would give me work in the factory if I took the children with me. A good friend of my husband, a weaver, had a little influence and gave me a little work as a warper...But how hard it was for me to keep the kids next to me. If they had been perfectly healthy, then it certainly wouldn't have been so difficult. Unfortunately, however, they had developed scrofula and used to tear their skin off in pieces. But the man who made sure that I was given work was a very good person and took care of the children a little so that they didn't tear the skin off their heads and faces.

The man's name was *Leybe der Vashelkover [the Vashlikover]*. He lived in Vashelkove [Vashlikov] but weaved in Bialystok...He did me many favors. He was such a good person...My husband used to write to him. If I wanted to know what was new with him, I would go to him [Leybe] and ask him and he would tell me everything. But my husband never wrote to me except on Passover or Sukkot, when he wrote a few words and sent five dollars. But he didn't send more than five dollars,

(Page 98)

and this only once or twice a year. When he didn't feel like it, he didn't write at all. So three anxious years passed...

A great misfortune struck us at that time, and my brother died quite suddenly. It was not known whether he himself had turned on the gas, or whether the flame had gone out (and the gas continued to flow out]. Anyway, when they found him, he was already dead. Well, the misfortune affected my brother Notke in such a way that he became very ill and could no longer work...Before that, he had sent me quite a few money, and after that, no more money could be sent to me at all...For a long time, I was in great pain until he got well again...I had almost nothing at all to eat for myself and my children, and had to borrow or lend everything, and when I got a little work, I paid it back...

A long time passed like that. I worked and hoped that he would send me something from America and I could pay my debts. But the grocer already knew what had happened in our family and began to dither. When I took some goods again and had no money, she said that it was too much, I couldn't clean out her store. I asked her to be patient, because I would get a few rubles from America and I would pay her back immediately.

Because of my daughters' scrofula disease, I had to go to the hospital. I could not afford a doctor whom I would have had to pay. There were doctors working in the hospital who were acquaintances of mine. They did their best for me and my children. They wrote prescriptions for me to get free medicine and olive oil in view of my children's scrofula disease.

At home it was bitterly cold and I had no money to buy a cart of wood. I had to get it from the "tsdoke" (in America we say charity)...Now you know how I suffered for the three years when my husband was in America...every now and then I wrote to him and described my agony, but he pretended not to know anything...

57.

But things turned out well for me. Not far from Bialystok, two miles away, is a shtetl, Vashilkove [Vashlikov]. And from Vashlikov three girls came to me to rent a room.

(Page 99)

Well, I didn't have a separate room for them, but my "fale" (here we call it front room) was very big, and next to the door, where you went in, there was another little chamber, just for one girl. So two girls could sleep together with me and the daughters, and one slept in the little chamber. The girls belonged to the "Profes", they were members of Polish associations. They made sure that the work in the factories should be distributed equally to all the workers. At that time there were no trade unions. Those who were more appreciated by the factory owner or worked faster got more work. The members of the "Profes" made sure that the work was distributed fairly. They used to go to the factory owner and threaten that if he did not establish a fair order in the factory, they would take the workers away from him and make sure that he did not get any other workers either. The factory owner was then usually frightened and instructed his master to distribute the work equally to each employee, otherwise he would regret it...

I too was affected by this. Sometimes I only got a few orders a week to prepare warp yarn tapes, sometimes more. As a result, the girls who lived with me went to the supervisors of their association. They then asked the master [of my factory] if one warper was not enough for all the work that needed to be done? If not, that is, if she could not do all the work alone, the master would have to give me half of her job. The master was not harmed by the fact that I got a little more work, it did not affect his position, but it stung him like with knives that people could come and influence him, although it was not their own factory. He said to me and the regular warper that he had been given an order to divide up the work. If he did not do this, they would kill him. And, after all, he was the father of children and had a wife. The other girl, that is, the other warper, also belonged to the association. In the past, she had watched to prepare as many warp yarn tapes as possible, but now she didn't argue about it anymore and accepted the matter unmoved. For the master, however, this was as if his life had been taken away from him...A little later it was forgotten and he got so used to it that he already took care all by himself to divide the work equally for everyone...

Now a better time was already dawning for me. My girls had grown up and used to go for walks in the forest with other children.

(Page 100)

Everything was looking much better, and I even tried to save a few rubles to go to America...

I did not know what had happened to my brother Alter. It happened that a gypsy woman came to me at my workplace and asked me to let her read my cards. I allowed it, and the gypsy told me that one of my brothers had died in America. She asked me: "You have a brother in America, don't you?" Perhaps someone had told her...Many in the factory knew that my brother Alter had died. Alter's wife, Sore, had worked in the same factory before she went to America. Sore had family friends in the factory, and they all knew...I think they had sent the gypsy woman to tell me...

I then went straight to my cousin's house. She lived on Nowolipie [Lipowa Street] and had a large men's goods store there. I asked her which of my brothers had died, but she wouldn't tell me. Her husband had returned from America a few months earlier and she knew from him that none of my family had died. However, my brother Note had been ill, and therefore he had not written to me.

I did not believe my cousin. I had an uncle, *Rakhmil*, who worked in a field making soap. I went to him and asked: "Which one of my brothers died?" And he told me that my brother Alter had died and what had happened. My uncle's wife was a sister of Alter's wife, *Sore [Sara]*. I had known before that Alter had been very sick. He had not wanted to be drafted into the Russian military service at that time, after all, and had done himself harm. He was frail, and the illness tormented him so much that he no longer wanted to live. He saw how the young people were all working, and he himself was so sick. The doctors forbade him to work in the factory. He was a silk weaver. His wife Sore already had children, two boys, but the younger of the two died when he was one year old. The older boy was called *Luie* [1], after my father Leybe...When my brother Alter could no longer work

(Page 101)

in the factory, he bought a store, a small grocery...The weavers had formed an association, and if something happened to a member, they helped each other. They undertook to help Alter. Their help consisted of buying whatever they needed from Alter's store. Alter's and Sore's compatriots also bought from them...

But they both had to work long hours during the day, so they took turns. Early in the morning he went to the store, later in the day she came to relieve him, and in the evening they both served their customers. What exactly happened to him, we do not know.

58.

I forgot to tell you that when Mushe was seven years old, I always prepared something to cook before I went to work. She, Mushe, was already cooking and her younger sister was helping...At home, however, there were not such stoves as in America; there was only a small stove ("oyvele") like a plate that stood on a small table. Mushe did not find it difficult to put the pot to cook [on the stove]. But once when she wanted to skim off the pot, she was not careful and burned her whole face.

Imagine how I suffered back then. But time does not stand still. My girls grew up, and a Jewish school was founded in Bialystok. I dressed up my girls in the most beautiful clothes, with brown skirts, red blouses and black aprons, and sent them to school. Their scrofula disease had healed and they were very beautiful girls...

---

[1] According to family lore, he was called Leib.

Meanwhile, the revolution had broken out in Russia. It was 1905. The master, his name was *Shmuel*, came to the factory and loudly announced that everyone should go home. He assumed that we would not be able to come home later. It was in the evening ["farnakht"] at four o'clock. We heard that one was going to open the prison and free the prisoners...

I hurried home, because I lived not far from the prison...Just as I left the factory yard, I saw that my

(Page 102)

master, *Shmuel*, was also leaving the yard, and his uncle, Preyzman, was following him, shouting that he should not go any further because he would be shot at. The prison would be opened even without him. But the master answered his uncle that he wanted to watch and would be right back...

When he reached the prison, the place was already full of soldiers. The socialists and the revolutionaries actually opened the gates of the prison, and immediately the soldiers started shooting. My master Shmuel was the first to be shot. Many more innocent people were shot...I still remember his funeral. I too went to the cemetery. It was only a small funeral procession, only his family walked behind, because they were afraid of an attack...

I remember how his uncle cried...his uncle was already an old man, about 75 years. He was the brother of Shmuel's mother, the richest man in Bialystok. Everyone knew the Preyzmans. The family mourned greatly. Shmuel left behind his wife with three small children. He was a very capable man and the head of all the departments in the factory. He had joined his uncle in the factory as a boy of 15 and had learned the weaving trade, after which he worked his way up to master and became the boss of the whole factory...After Shmuel's death, his brother, *Mikhl*, became the supervisor of the factory...

It was not possible to walk in the streets, because they were guarded for a long time by the military and also by the cossacks with bare swords. We were afraid to go to work. We walked in the side streets...The situation continued for a long time...

When it became quieter, we began to feel freer again. We went for a walk in Saxon Garden again. I remember my two girls walking with many neighborhood children in the urban gardens and through Sarazer [Surasker] Street.

On Surasker Street workers used to gather and hold meetings...Once, the police were shooting and many young people were injured, the others were arrested. This was on a Shabbat evening. My children came running home terrified...

(Page 103)

And so the shootings continued and we were again afraid to walk in the streets. So it went on since the Christian New Year until Shavuot. The whole world learned about the great and sad pogrom in Bialystok, and even today it is known.

59.

I remember how frightened the new master, *Mikhl,* was and how he exclaimed in a tearful voice: "Go home as soon as possible, there is a pogrom against the Jews!"

The hooligans were already in the "New Town", ran to the hospital and murdered all the Jews who were there. They killed all the Jewish doctors and nurses, and all the Jewish patients who were still there...

It had been a Christian holiday, and the Christians had gone in procession. A [provocateur] had been sent to the roof to shoot into the crowd, and he shot a participant in the procession. It was a planned thing to have an excuse to kill Jews...

There was a rich family called *"the Lapiduses."* They owned a cloth factory and had sons and daughters, eight children in all, all educated. Their children had just gone to the New Town to watch the procession...Several of the sons were shot soon after. They had still run into the courtyard of the hospital, but the "pogromshtshikes" [the pogromists] ran after them and shot them...

In the hospital worked a man named *Shloymke the Feldsher*. He was a very pleasant man who served all the people who came to the hospital. The pogromists killed Shloymke, and the whole town and all the surrounding small towns mourned him. He left behind a wife with four small children...

On "Varshever Gas" [Warszawa Street] the pogromists ran from house to house, broke open the gates and killed whoever they came across...

And now I will tell you about myself. Just as the master had come to us in the factory to send us all home, I began to run home. I had to cross an empty field and I began to run faster.

(Page 104)

I wore a headscarf with black and white squares. I pulled it deep into my face so that I would not be recognized as a Jew. The field was next to the prison. When I was already next to the prison, I saw the pogromists, not far from me...I was already next to Vashlikover Gas [Wasilkowska Street], about 50 feet away. But they didn't recognize me because I was covering my face with my headscarf...

I ran to my children, but I did not meet them at home...There was a good and pious woman, called *Leye*, whose children used to play mine. She had taken my children to her home, knowing that I was at work. She would not let them outside until I came to pick them up...When I brought my children home, there was terror and fear.

When I arrived home with my children, the girls who stayed with me told me that all the neighbors of our yard had gone to the landlord in whose apartments we all lived. He was a German and the government made sure he was spared.

We did not feel like eating. We ran hungry and full of fear to our landlord and stayed there until late at night...The German owned apartments and large stone houses, including two courtyards with houses...We were six neighbors, all Jews, and lived in one courtyard, and in the second courtyard all tenants were also Jews. We hid at our landlord's and stayed there until 12 midnight...

60.

When it became quiet, everyone went to their homes, hungry and scared. Who knew what would happen during the night and whether we would still be alive and up the next morning...

The night remained quiet. Everyone crept out to buy something from the baker, because maybe later they would not have the opportunity. But the baker had not baked, there were only leftovers from Thursday, but at least you could get something for the children.

(Page 105)

Friday morning at ten o'clock we heard shooting and screaming again. Well, what should we do with the children now? Where could we hide them? We went to the landlord. But he had already repented of his behavior and was not letting anyone in...So we consulted where we could hide our children, because the pogromists were not far from us...

We were in a wide street, the "Vashlikover Gas" [Wasilkowska Street], a boulevard. Horse-trams were moving on the street, and opposite, on the other side of the street, lived a rich owner of some stone houses. Officers lived in these houses. I ran with my children to the owner, a Jew, to ask him to let us in. The yard in question was screened off from the pogromists, for soldiers stood guard at the gates...

But it was already too late. They wouldn't let me and my children in because there were already too many people there...What could I do now? I saw other women taking their children to the baker. The baker let all the children in and put them on his oven; it was a big oven...

The "self-defense" arrived at the baker's, young people who were ready to shoot if the pogromists approached the bakery...

Two hundred feet away, the hooligans were already pogroming the poor stores. They robbed all the merchandise, leaving none of those they found in the yard or in the store alive. They also took the pillows and feather beds, everything that was left, including bed covers, they crushed and let the feathers blow out with the wind, and the whole street was full of feathers...

I stood at the window and watched. The Polish hooligans broke the doors and windows of the Jewish stores with iron bars. The hooligans had no fear, because the officers had told the pogromists that they had the right to do with the Jews as they pleased...

61.

Next to us they did not shoot...I already wrote that officers lived across the street, and where I lived the landlord was a German, and thus, as they say in America,

(Page 106)

"a citizen". In other houses, the Jews put crosses in the windows, borrowed from their good gentile friends...

After the pogromists had run riot on our street, they went through other streets and came to "Nowolipie Gas" [Lipowa Street]. There they grabbed everyone they could get. They stormed the apartments, there was a father with his son, the son stood protectively in front of his father, and so they shot them both.

They grabbed little children and ripped out their tongues. I looked through the window and saw this with my own eyes! It was Friday morning. Friday night they raged on and marched through our street again, "Unter der Turme" [Behind the Prison]. They saw me from far away. What was I to do now? There was no place to hide anymore. As I wrote before, girls from Vashlikove were staying with me. They were working in the factories. They were joined by young boys whom they knew, they were from the "self-defense". They already knew that soon the pogromists would come...The boys from "self-defense" advised me to go to the opposite side of the street and ask the landlord of the stone houses, a Jew, to ask the soldiers to let me and the children in. In his stone houses the pogromists would not shoot because officers lived there. But just as I came to the man, and had not yet spoken a single word, they began shooting into the windows. All those who had been there, men and women, were already lying together under the beds...The pogromists had forgotten that officers lived there in the buildings, and they shot, but they didn't hit anyone...

The owner of the stone houses came running into the yard and asked a soldier to take me across the street, and sure enough, the soldier took me across. I had covered my head with a headscarf...It was on Friday evening. When I crossed the street, there were shot Jews lying there...I met my children alive, thank God. They were hiding under the beds with the girls.

In our house one had not shot because, as I wrote earlier, the owner was a German. The fellows from self-defense were

(Page 107)

ready to shoot at the pogromists if they stormed into our house.

On the same street, not far from us, was a "tartak," which in America is a "lumberyard". Many people gathered there. It was already very late at night when the pogromists stormed into the lumberyard and killed sixteen people...

Not far from the lumberyard lived a family. The man had returned from America not long ago. He, his pregnant wife with their small child were also hiding in the lumberyard. The man was holding the child on his knees. They [the pogromists] took the child from him, handed it to his wife and shot him. The wife asked to be shot as well, but the murderers did not want that. The man had shown them his papers beforehand that he was an American citizen, but they didn't even want to look at the papers...

The news about the pogrom in Bialystok spread all over the world. The newspapers wrote about it all over Russia and abroad...The superiors [representatives] of the Russian Jews turned to America with the request to stop the pogrom. America then issued a "prikaz" (decree) that if Russia did not stop the pogrom within 24 hours, America would annul the treaty with Russia. Russia was frightened and immediately stopped the pogroms...

62.

On Shabbat morning we already knew that the pogrom had come to a halt and we breathed more freely...I opened a window and saw the shot people lying in the street being collected. They were being taken away on large carts. I lamented and cried a lot...

Since it was Shabbat, and one is not allowed to work on Shabbat, the Rov [the Rabbi] had issued the decision that, exceptionally, the murdered people could be collected. They were taken to the courtyard of the hospital and laid there...On Sunday morning, everyone went to the courtyard of the

(Page 108)

hospital...May it never happen again that we have to look at something like this. There, spread out on straw, lay 160 dead people. The hospital was full of wounded people. I came back from the hospital with loose hair, which I tore out.[1]

On Monday, people from all over the city went to the funeral. First the murdered little children were carried, then the adults...All the victims were buried in the cemetery in a collective grave, even the little children...On top of the pit a large brick wall [2] was errected, on which the names of each victim were written...

My mother lived in Krynki, six miles from Bialystok, and when she heard about the pogrom, she came immediately. She had already been informed that her son, Alter, had died in America. Filled with pain, she took me and the children to Krynki. Her second husband took me and my children very kindly...However, I stayed in Krynki only briefly, only a week...After all, I had to go to work, and the children did not want to stay with my mother without me.

When I came back from Krynki with the kids, the fright was still deep. People were still afraid to go out on the street...When we went to the factory, we went through the side streets...On the main streets there were cossacks with bare swords. My girls went to school through other streets...

When I went home from the factory in the evening, I ran out of strength worrying about seeing them alive again...

My younger girl, Libele, came down with measles. One night, as I was preparing supper, there was shooting again! I took my two girls and ran out with them behind the house. My Libele was full of measles spots. Who had shot? A gentile lout and a young Christian woman had gone out of control and wanted to scare everyone...

---

[1] a gesture of mourning, the "hair sacrifice".

[2] literally "a moyer with a groyser vant" = a building made of bricks with a big wall. However, I have based my translation on the lore of Rachel's family.

My older girl, Mushe, got sick from all the horrors. For whole a week she wouldn't eat. One had to open her mouth and put some food in it, but she just wouldn't swallow it. She was already so sick that I ran to Doctor *Khazanovitsh*, who lived on Nowolipie [Lipowa Street].

Memorial Pillar in Bialystok with the victim's names of the 1906 pogrom [possibly also including the names of the 1905 pogrom described by Rachel]. Old photos, courtesy of Dr. Tomek Wisniewski.

(Page 109)

Khazanovitsh was a good doctor, but also very quick-tempered. I did not leave his house until he went with me in the cab to my house. But he was so quick-tempered that he already wanted to hit me, he shouted at me and wanted to hit me; he was always so quick-tempered, but this time more than usual.

63.

When the news got around in America about what was happening in Bialystok, my brother Note went from Paterson to New York to see my husband. He urged him to help his family, that is, me and the children, to get across. He [my husband] showed some mercy and sent me a little money. My brother Note also laid out a little money for me and sent a ship's ticket...

I was already preparing to go to America when my husband sent me a letter telling me not to go, that it would calm down with time, and then he would come back home. But I did not believe him and did not inquire with him anymore. I ordered an agent to provide me and the children with a governor's passport.

After I paid off all my debts, I had no money left over on the trip. I was not able to pay rent to my landlord. I owed him 36 rubles for 12 months. I sold the few pieces of furniture I had for 12 rubles. As I have already written, the landlord was a German. On the first day of the pogrom he let the Jewish neighbors in to hide. On the second day, however, he regretted it and did not let anyone in. Therefore, I didn't worry about not paying him the rent...If I had the money, I would have paid it to him so that he shouldn't speak badly about Jews...But God knew that I really didn't have a ruble left on the way for me and the children...

My mother came from Krynki to say goodbye to me. She gave me three rubles. She could have given me more, but it would have been from her second husband, and she was not allowed to give money from him...

I missed my ship. I had to postpone the trip for a whole week...

(Page 110)

The children were sick (only) for a few days. They went to the first class, where the rich people were, and these gave them nibbles...It was really bad to travel such a long distance and have no money. The trip took three weeks...

First, a small ship took us to Liverpool. There we waited for ten days for the big ship. We stayed in a hostel at the expense of the shipping company. But without money I could not give my children any pleasure at all. At least we were happy that there was no pogrom on the streets...The children livened up ...

Once, it happened that my children got lost in Liverpool. But in Liverpool there were many Frenchmen, good people, and they brought the children back to the hostel. The French already thought that my girls lived in the hostel for emigrants.

A stupid story happened to me as well. I did not have my luggage with me. While we took our seats in the small ship, my luggage was going to New York on another ship. However, I did not know that. I went to the arrival point of the ships, they took me to all the places, but I couldn't find my luggage anywhere. I also didn't know how to get back to the hostel and which "konke" [horse-tram] to take. I also didn't have any money with me. I stood there in despair, what could I do? I could not speak [the language] either. But a man came up to me and asked what I wanted. I showed him the address. Then he took me to the "konke" that went to the hostel, told the conductor to let me out at the hostel, and paid for me...When I got home, I met my children all teary-eyed. They didn't know what was going on...

64.

Finally the big ship came from London to Liverpool, and we left for New York. What we had to endure! The winds were so violent that the ship was tossed up and down, and we saw nothing but sky and water. We thought we would never see land again and would have to stay on the water forever...

(Page 111)

When it was calm and there was no wind, the sky contrasted so beautifully and blue against the water. It was a pleasure to look at this beauty of the sky and water...And when the sun cast its rays into the water, the beauty of the sight was so magnificent that I cannot describe it. And at night, when the moon and the stars shone on the sea, the eyes could not get enough of what beauty was reflected on the water...

But when the wind came up, we were terrified on the deck...It happened at night that the sailors woke us all up. We were told to leave the cabins as quickly as possible and go out on deck, because one side of the ship was full of water... They managed to pump out the water and save the people from drowning. We had all run out of the cabins naked and barefoot, and the children were terrified...The storm lasted longer than a night and a day. We, the people on the ship, no longer expected to stay alive. But a great miracle happened, the wind calmed down, and everyone praised God...

We arrived in America alive. I and the children were taken to Boston. Why, you ask, to Boston? Because I was afraid to declare that my husband would pick me and the children up from the ship. After all, he didn't want us to go to America. He would be angry and send us back...Before I left for America, I wrote a letter to my husband saying that I was afraid to stay in Bialystok because, God forbid, another pogrom might follow. I also wrote him that I could work in America, and he should not worry. I would be able to stand on my own feet and help him make a living. He should just be good to me and the children...

My husband was working in Englewood at the time, making children's pants. My brother Ishye knew where my husband worked. He went to Englewood and wanted to give him money to pick me up from the ship. My husband refused the money and immediately drove to Boston to pick us up. My children and I arrived the night before Yom Kippur at the Boston "Kesl-Gardn" [Castle-Garden][1]...I remember how we all got a good meal...

(Page 112)

In the middle of the day of Yom Kippur, the officials of the "castle-garden" came in to me and said: "Your husband is very happy that you are here with the children. He already wanted to meet with you, but he can't see you until tomorrow morning because we don't let passengers out on Yom Kippur...". The people who had seen my husband in the courtyard of "castle-garden" spoke to me because I had such a handsome husband who was so happy that I and the children were now in America. He looked like a good and happy man...

---

[1] "Kesl-Gardn"= Castle Garden. Until 1890, immigrants to the United States were received and registered at "Castle Garden," at the southern tip of Manhattan. Apparently, this term became so ingrained that it was sometimes later used as a synonym for a receiving station.

Yom Kippur fell on a Shabbat at that time. On Sunday, early in the morning, I prettied up my girls, dressed them in beautiful clothes, black skirts with red blouses, and braided red ribbons with big bows in their braids...And when my husband saw them, he held them in his arms for several minutes and couldn't get enough of them, they looked so beautiful...

65.

My husband took us to a ship that was going to Paterson. He bought us bananas and tomatoes, but we didn't know what to eat it with, so we didn't want to eat it. But he taught us how to eat it...

I cried a lot. When we were riding in the ship, he asked me why I was crying so much. I told him that I was crying for my brother Alter, who had died. He then said to me that he had been with my sister, Sheyne Gitl, who was called *Gosye* in America. She had not cried at all, all the sadness just weighed so heavily on me...

He took us to my brother, Ishye. His wife, *Rokhel*, was a good, beautiful and fine woman. We had been very good friends even before my brother married her. She took me in very kindly. My brother, Notke, lived with my brother, Ishye...

Not far from my brother lived my sister, Sheyne Gitl, and she soon joined us as well. My sister-in-law, Rokhl [Rachel], cooked a fine lunch

(Page 113)

and in the evening my husband went back to Englewood...After a week he came to visit us and said we would live together as soon as he could get a room. He really didn't earn much, but we would make it work...

He rented a large room from a woman and took me and the children to Englewood. I was allowed to cook and eat in the kitchen, and the landlady taught me how to cook the American way...

Not two weeks passed and my husband read in the newspaper that they were looking for a contractor for children's pants in a large factory. So my husband immediately went to New York and signed a contract. He had a few hundred dollars and arranged quite a few machines, hired operators and a cutter, and did not do badly. He made a fine living and was even able to work independently.

We rented an apartment at 322 Essex Street, on the third floor, and bought some used furniture. The apartment was not bad. It was a large room with a small closet behind the door. My husband brought in a lodger, his cousin's son, his name was *Zalmen*. He was a very decent young man, but a bit sick.

Nine months later I gave birth to a girl, a great beauty. I gave her the name *Gosi*. It looked like everything was going to be fine and dandy now...My husband was so proud of the baby. He went out and bought a beautiful stroller. The other two girls were jealous of the little girl, they looked at her angrily and sometimes they even gave her a little slap...

My husband did not give me much money, only five dollars a week. He paid the rent for the apartment and bought things for the children...I was happy that I had given birth to such a beautiful girl, someone should try to imitate me...I was happy about my luck, that I had saved myself from the pogroms with my children and had a third child, and that my husband provided for our living.

(Possibly) Rachel with her three daughters,
photo courtesy of her grandson, Dr. Norton Snyder

Rachel with her three daughters, photo courtesy of Rachel's grandson, Dr. Norton Snyder

(Page 114)

66.

My joy lasted barely two years, before everything took a turn for the worse, and was no longer good at all...My husband fell out with the foreman, he even fought with him and tore his shirt to pieces...you will understand that he quit his job after that...

You ask what he did after that? He went away to Paterson, rented an apartment for me and the children, then left us there to go to New York alone. He toiled away in New York, and I toiled away in Paterson. I couldn't earn anything, because I had a small child after all. Why did he take me to Paterson? He wanted to take revenge on my family, he said, because I had come to America...

He had saved up three hundred dollars, one hundred dollars was already spent when he came with us to Paterson...In New York he couldn't get a job. So he started making children's pants on his own and taking them to Paterson to sell, but it wasn't enough to make a living...He tried to sew children's pants in Paterson, bought scraps of fabric for that, cut them on his own and sewed them together, and I helped him, but the situation was not good...

So he went back to New York, whirled around, but barely earned anything for himself. My children and I had nothing to eat and no money for apartment rent...so I was terminated. It was, I think, on a Shabbat when people from the court came and gave me a document that I had to move out. I lived on Voder Street [Water Street] after that. When on Shabbat my husband came and saw what had happened and that we needed a new apartment, he ran to look for something and rented three dark rooms on North-West Street, on the second floor. The bedroom was very small. You couldn't put more than a small bed in it, and it didn't have a window. And you know what he did? There was a window in the larger room, but he had nailed it shut, so it got damp in the apartment and we all became sick. For this small apartment was to pay eight rubles [1] rent a month, but even this money we did not have...

(Page 115)

I began to rack my brains as to what I could do to earn a living. My brothers had very good friends, silk manufacturers. One of them was named *Finklshteyn [Finkelstein]*. His associate was called *Daymant [Diamant]*, and the two of them taught me to "pikn"[2] silk pieces...My mother, may she rest in peace, looked after my little child and cooked for all of us. My mother did not live with me, but with my brother Notke. He had married a woman shortly before who was also a weaver, so they were both weaving. My mother cooked dinner for my family and we would meet to eat in my little apartment...

---

[1] It can be assumed that she means "dollars".
[2] pikn/oppikn shtiker zayd= I think that this term might be about cutting pieces of silk, and cleaning up the finished cut pieces at the edge.

67.

It would have been good if I and my children had not gotten sick from the bad apartment. Since I was not at home during the day, I did not pay close attention to what was happening to the children. One day, on a Shabbat, I took a look at Mushe and saw that her right armpit was hanging down and the whole shoulder was deformed, oh, I felt so scared! What could I do? I called my sister-in-law to me. She soon came, and I showed her what had happened to my Mushe. She immediately ran with me to an eminent bone doctor, and he said that she had consumption of the bones...He instructed her to wear a steel brace for two years and promised us that after the two years she would be healthy...

I also became ill and could no longer go to the "shap" [factory] and work. So I asked Mister Finklshteyn to give me the silk pieces to take home to "pikn" them there. And he actually gave them to me...But it was hard to carry the silk pieces together with the rollers. So I asked him to give me the silk without the rollers. However, I could not carry the silk pieces even without the rollers. As a result, early in the morning, before they went to school, my children would carry the finished silk pieces to the factory and bring new pieces so that I could "pikn" them...My older girl, who had fallen ill, was getting better, and she was already thirteen years old. Libe was eleven years old. My Libele checked the finished pieces that I had "opgepikt" and helped me "pikn" the new ones that she brought with her sister when they came from school...

(Page 116)

In this way we toiled for several years. Such young children had to drag pieces of silk from the factory early in the morning, in heavy frost and deep snow. Even to drive a dog outside would have been a shame...

We could not make a living from "pikn" silk. Society Ladies found out about us and gave me two dollars every two weeks for milk...I remember how embarrassed I was to go to them for the two dollars. It was just Hanukkah. Therefore, they gave me 4 dollars, 2 for milk and 2 dollars of Hanukkah money for my two daughters...

My children were very sick. My little Gosi got sick and we didn't know how to help the child. But a miracle happened. A farmer who brought me milk every morning came and saw that my Gosile could not breathe. He said, "Quick, call a doctor!" We immediately sent for a doctor, and she could barely be saved...

Our compatriots knew that I and my children were sick. They arranged for an "undertaking", and this brought in sixty dollars, besides sending us to Liberty[1]...

68.

We were in Liberty for six weeks. I cooked myself. My daughters had no more with them than one dress each. Every day I got up early in the morning and washed and ironed the clothes, and when my daughters came into the hall where all the summer guests gathered, they looked better and more beautiful than the children of the rich. I am not exaggerating, they were the most beautiful children there where we stayed.

Every morning I went to the farm where the cows were milked and gave the children fresh milk. They actually recovered very well...

To this day, I don't know which of my compatriots had been so good to me, and had arranged the six-week shipment to Liberty for the summer retreat. The children really came home much healthier and fresher than they had been before at Paterson...

(Page 117)

I wrote to my husband that we were coming home. He was in New York all the time...We met him at home. A little later he read in the paper that a factory for children's pants was opening in Paterson. Well, that was great joy that he would now stay home with us and work, and I would no longer have to depend on the two dollars for milk from the Society Ladies...

---

[1] note of Susan Pasquariella: There were 2 sanitoria that were established in Liberty, New York, in the early 1900s. One was the Loomis Sanitorium and the other was established by the Workmen's Circle, a leading Jewish Fraternal Association. See https://www.townofliberty.org/about/history/

Listen to what happened. The superiors of the Charity Society summoned my husband to their office and confronted him why he did not pay attention to his family. He told them that he had no earnings and was not healthy himself. They said that they wanted to see that he got a better job where he earned more. However, he should make sure that his family does not have to rely on charity. He promised them that he would do the best for his family...

He earned 16 dollars a week [1], but he was incredibly hot tempered. There were arguments over everything he didn't like. But in general I felt better and I didn't have to go to the charity anymore...

I myself earned money with "pikn" silk, and if my husband had not been so hot tempered, we would have got along well...

Not far from us lived a man who worked with him in the same factory. They used to go to and from work together. In the process, my husband spread all kinds of things about me...He was angry with my mother, which is why she had to live with strangers. My brother Notke had become ill with lung disease and had to go to California, so unfortunately my mother had to live with strangers...

69.

Before my brother went to California, he had lived on "Circle Avenue", on a mountain, and had five rooms. We took over the apartment. I did write that we lived on Northwest Street, very poorly, in three small rooms with one window, on the second floor. And we had all become ill there from the living conditions...

(Page 118)

Downstairs had lived a drunken German. He had a daughter of 21 and an adolescent son. Once when he was drunk, he wanted to kill his daughter and son. They hid with us, because the German did not dare to come over to us...

---

[1] Here's a little mental leap. Apparently, he was actually given a job.

When my brother Notke, his wife Flore [1] and their three-month-old child left for Los Angeles, my husband took over the apartment. We bought the furniture and lived in a posh apartment...My husband and I worked and we could already pay the rent...

When everything was proving to be fine, a new problem arose. I had already been sick for a long time, and now my Gosile also became ill and contracted pneumonia that would not heal...I myself was yellow as wax. Everyone who knew me was worried about the fate of the three poor children because their mother looked so yellow. I had to go to the doctor with my child, and her father had to carry her in his arms to do so. However, she did not allow this and screamed...Thereupon, my husband was very angry with me, I would incite the children against him, so that they did not even want to be carried by him...My husband did not want me to carry her, because he was afraid that the dragging would harm me...

When my Gosi was three years old, she had recovered, and I had also become healthier. Life improved, we didn't fight so much anymore...

When my Gosile was four years old, I sent her to kindergarten, which was not far from our house. From the very beginning she brought me little paper cut-out toys.

---

[1] According to family lore, she was also called "Faiga".

(Page 119)

70.

And do you know what my Gosile used to do after school? She went to the Voder Street [Water Street], far from home. Meetings were held there by the weavers who were on strike. At that time, "*Haywood* the *Great*"[1] agitated the weavers to strike for better working conditions. The movement included a woman, "*Beth Flynn*,"[1] who organized the workers. My little daughter liked her very much...[The first time] we didn't know where she had gone, and when we came home from work and couldn't find her, we couldn't sit quietly at home...

We looked for her everywhere for many hours, and could not find her until we learned that she was at Water Street. Later we already knew where to find her...

Once, when she did not come home, she became dehydrated and her lungs were attacked. I noticed that something was wrong with the girl and went with her to the doctor. The doctor paid attention to our whole family, including my brother and sister...The doctor knew that Gosile had pneumonia when she was one and a half years old. The doctor examined her and found out that she suffered from severe bronchitis...Since he knew the entire family, he also knew about everyone's illnesses, and also that my brother Notke was in California. He himself had sent my brother Notke to California to cure his lung disease. Now the doctor said to me that I must go to California to save my child...

---

[1] "Big Bill" Haywood (William Dudley) and Beth Flynn (Elizabeth Gurley Flynn) were leaders of the Industrial Workers of the World (IWW), see https://en.wikipedia.org/wiki/Bill_Haywood
https://en.wikipedia.org/wiki/Elizabeth_Gurley_Flynn

When I got home and told my husband what the doctor had said, he didn't believe me and went to see him himself. The doctor scared him even more and told him that it was absolutely necessary to go to California with the child. But we didn't have any money. So I went to my brother Ishye, in New York, and asked him to lend me 50 dollars. But my brother didn't have that much money either. He was a poor Jew, he had to work very hard to support his family. He delivered bread, challah, rolls and bagels to the houses...he had a wife and four children. The apartment rent

(Page 120)

in New York was very expensive, and the children also had to be clothed. His wife had a small embroidery business. They both worked, but they were not lucky. My brother was very distressed that he could not help me at all. He had 16 dollars that had accumulated from his pastry delivery service and gave it to me.

I felt so miserable that I had emptied my brother's pockets...My husband went to the office [of the factory], where he worked, and told there that his child was sick and his wife had to go to California with her. The office boss called the doctor, and he confirmed that it was the truth. As a result, the boss lent my husband quite a few dollars, which he deducted from his weekly salary...

71.

In Los Angeles, my sister Sheyne Gitl lived with her husband, and they already had a son of eight years...When my brother Notke went to Los Angeles, he only had his three-month-old son with him. But now he already had two boys. The first one was called *Louie* [1], the second *Moyshe*. He was one and a half years old and such a beautiful child, a blond with long, curly hair...He was as tall as a three-year-old child.

---

[1] From the family side it is said that he was called "Leib".

I went to my brother Note, and my brother and his wife received me very kindly. But the kindness of my sister-in-law Flore, may she rest in peace, did not last long...I tried to do everything for the peace of the house, but I fell out of favor with my sister-in-law and she just could not see me anymore...

What should I do now with the sick child; I myself was not healthy either. I tried to find some work, but there was none in my trade...I did not want to be dependent on my brother and my sister...Rich women used to come in to my brother's house to buy dairy products...He delivered butter, cheese and other food to the houses. He led a nice life.

(Page 121)

He could not do any other work, because he came as a lung patient, but when he drove around outside in the air, he felt better.

Among the women who came in to my brother to buy dairy products was a woman named *Lize*, she was a very good one. I had a talk with her. She told me that she had worked in a factory where they sold new cloaks; her boss had fallen in love with her and they got married...I told her about my bitter life, that I had left my husband and the two girls back in Paterson and that my husband didn't earn much. He had to pay for the girls' upkeep, so he couldn't send anything. I asked her to do something for me...

Her husband's factory was located at 443 Spring Street. I lived on Boyle Heights [1]. She asked the foreman of the factory to teach me how to line the suits and coats. I learned it very quickly and made six dollars the first week. I left my daughter when she was still asleep. Next to our apartment was a school, and my sister-in-law prepared breakfast for her. Gosile went to school and usually came back to the house at 12 o'clock to eat lunch...

At the beginning it went very well, but a little later she drove me out of the house. She used to tell my brother that he could give me as much money as he wanted, but she didn't want me in the house...I got sick, it was on Shabbat night. I suffered from bronchitis and coughed very violently all night...

My sister, Sheyne Gitl came to my brother's house every Sunday for lunch, along with her husband and two boys...My sister-in-law cooked the best lunch for her, her husband and her children. [But] she blasphemed about me to my sister. I cried [and asked my sister], "What should I do with my little child?" My sister answered me: "Do you want Note to divorce his wife because of you?"

Not far from my sister-in-law lived my friend's sister, *Eyde [Ida] Miller*, and she said to me: "Just get away from Flore, and you'll get healthy, too!" Not far from my brother there was a room for rent. Mrs. Miller went there with me and I rented a room. The landlady promised to cook for me and take care of my child...That came as requested, but it was no good. The landlady herself had a boy the same age

(Page 122)

as my Gosile, and he beat her...He was strong, and my girl was a weak one after all...

My landlady didn't have more children other than this boy, she was already middle-aged...Once, when the boy punched my girl in the chest, she punched back...No, there was no point anymore. When I got home from work, the landlady told me to move out...So I went away to see Mrs. Miller, and she told me that I could stay with her that night along with my daughter...

72.

There was an ironer named *Goldberg* who worked at the factory. I told him about my problems with my landlady, and he told me: "I have a room for you and when you get home from work tonight you can move in already. I won't rent it to you too expensive, my wife will cook for you and also take care of your child"...The room was next to Breed Street and across from the same school...They, [the Goldbergs], also had children going to school and they took my child with them.

---

[1] About Boyle Heights and its Jewish history, see:
https://www.laconservancy.org/jewish-american-heritage
https://scalar.usc.edu/hc/jewish-histories-boyle-heights/index

I didn't know how to thank God for delivering me from all these problems, from my sister-in-law, and from my bad landlady...When I came home from work in the evening, a hot meal was already prepared for me and my child, and Mrs. Goldberg took good care of my girl...

But when I had already got work, I became very ill, and Doctor Bless said that I had to have an operation, because I was suffering from a sagging of the upper bowel...So I went to the hospital, where a women's doctor came twice a week, who was a specialist in gynecological diseases. She said that I would still have time before surgery was needed. She treated me and I actually got better. I have not had any operation even to this day, and it was then in 1913.

My bronchitis had already gotten better, but I had a lot of grief, and I remember lying there at night

(Page 123)

coughing. I had to sleep next to the [open] window, with my head outside. I went to Doctor Bless and he said I must not go to work or I would get pneumonia...So I went to my place of work, a factory which was run by two shareholders, *Morris Sachs and Mister Katsop*. I told them that Doctor Bless had forbidden me to work because I was sick.

On North Broadway there was a big hospital with good doctors. I went to this hospital and there were really good doctors there; one of them, a specialist, examined me and had to laugh very hard at Doctor Bless and his statement that I should not work. He said to me that I just had a cold, gave me some medicine, and instructed me to come back in a week. Within the week I was feeling better and didn't need any more medicine. I was very worried about the fact that I had quit my job...So I went back to my employer and told him that I had made a big mistake quitting my job. I had only had a cold and it was now over. The employer, Mister Katsop, said that he was very happy that I was feeling better and I could go right back to work. I was so happy that I didn't know how to thank God...At that time I was already earning seven rubles a week...

73.

Well, and again problems came up. There were very few work assignments left, but I still had to send money to my children in Paterson. Meanwhile, an acquaintance came to me and asked me if I would work for two weeks with a "kimpetorin" [a woman who had just given birth]. I asked if I could come with my Gosile...My acquaintance asked the "kimpetorin", and she said yes. I had to work very hard at the "kimpetorin". There were four small children with her. Early in the morning I had to prepare breakfast for the woman and her four children, dress the children and send them to school...I had to make sure that the baby wraps were clean and also cook dinner for the whole

(Page 124)

family...The work was not as bad as the kids...They used to beat my daughter and did not let her eat or play.

I barely lasted the two weeks and made 45 dollars...I went to my sister Sheyne Gitel and asked her to lend me 50 dollars. She sent me to her husband at the store. Her husband answered me that he was not a bank...My sister and her husband were very rich. They had a big dry goods store on Ninth Street and Central Avenue. And when people have become rich, they become bad...I left my sister with a broken heart...I had to get my children out of Paterson. But what was I supposed to do now? My dear brother, Neyte [Note], was there for me. He took my 50 dollars and added another 50 dollars, and he sent the money to my husband in Paterson...

Mushe was seventeen years old and Libe was fourteen. Unfortunately, the hundred dollars was not enough to bring my family to Los Angeles. As a result, my husband went to New York to see my brother Ishye, and Ishye gave him, I think, fifty dollars. They could now come together with my mother...

About my mother, I would like to tell you the following: Before my brother Note went to California with his family, she was with him. Then she went to New York and stayed with my brother Ishye. She stayed with him for several months, but she did not get along with his children. My brother Ishye had a daughter named *Enye* and three boys. The older son, his name was *Louie*, was always angry with his grandmother because she was so pious and taught him "Jewishness". He was a young boy, maybe ten years old...

The other boys were still very small and obeyed her. The girl, she was already older, was very good to her grandma, that is, to my mother...My mother cooked for the whole family because my sister-in-law was not at home. She had an embroidery store after all and worked alone on a machine...

Before my mother came and lived with my sister-in-law, there was only one kind of cooking vessel in her home. When my mother came and lived with her, she bought separate cooking vessels for milk and for meat [according Jewish Law].

(Page 125)

But the children did not care. My mother couldn't stand it and told my sister-in-law. My sister-in-law, a very fine person, then gave her 5 dollars, and my mother went to Paterson...

After my brother Note and his family had already gone to California, my mother stayed with my sister, Sheyne Gitl. My sister and her husband were very good to her. He was a silk weaver and she used to "pikn" the silk. My mother looked after my sister's family...But it happened that my brother-in-law lost his job. Moreover, he was not a healthy man. Therefore, he wrote to my brother Note that he lost his job and could not find another one...My brother wrote him to sell everything and come to California, Los Angeles. So my sister went to Los Angeles with her husband and her boy (he was very naughty)...

My mother stayed in Paterson and rented a room with strangers. She couldn't stay with me because my husband didn't get along with her. He was constantly objecting to my mother...Besides, I had to go to Los Angeles. So I left my girls in Paterson with my husband, and my mother cooked for them and did everything for them. And by the time I went to catch up with my two girls, my mother had already arrived in Los Angeles with them...

74.

When the children from Paterson came to live with me, I lived in one room with my Gosile, who was five years old at the time. And now in addition, my mother and the two girls moved into that room. We slept on the floor until we got an apartment. And this apartment had four rooms, but what an apartment it was! The walls were not painted, there was no water for the bathtub. You had to warm the water, pour it [into the tub], and then scoop it out and pour it into the toilet...I was exhausted before I even started bathing the children...

(Page 126)

[We rented] the apartment from a gentile woman who didn't want to do anything for us. When we asked her to paint the apartment, she said, "If you don't like it like this, you can move out!". For the money we had to pay, we couldn't get another apartment, it cost $12 a month, so it was really very cheap, but even that money I couldn't pay for the poor apartment...

You couldn't enter the yard, it was all dirty and overgrown. We were afraid that mice would get into the house...The floor was pitted and black, there was no stove. We bought a stove and put it on two boxes, but we were afraid it would tip over with the pots...The little stove cost a dollar, so you can imagine what a cheap thing it was...And on that stove I had to heat water to bathe the children...

I didn't have any furniture. One Sunday my sister came and gave me a gold five dollar piece in a little scarf. My brother bought me furniture for fourteen dollars: an old bed and another bed that was already falling apart a bit, a table with drawers and a few old chairs painted white that you were afraid to sit on. We had no more than two chairs, and when visitors came, there were a few little boxes to sit on...With the seven dollars a week I earned, I had to live with my children and my mother, may she rest in peace...

My brother Note, may he rest in peace, delivered butter, cheese, milk, eggs and other food to the houses, and he did not abandon me...Twice a week he drove through the street where I lived, bringing me butter, cheese, milk and eggs and other food. It went on like this for a long time...

75.

A year later my husband came to Los Angeles but he did not know how to live. He couldn't find a job, he worked in the production of children's pants, but there was no such work here. He was only able to work a little bit as an iron junk dealer, but he earned very little...

(Page 127)

I remember sitting in the factory one lunchtime eating. An operator came up to me and told me my husband was waiting for me. I quickly ran down on the street. He [my husband] told me I wouldn't be happy about what he was going to tell me. He would have to go back to Paterson or to New York. There was no point in struggling here anymore, he couldn't earn anything here. I then cried bitterly, and he said: "I know you are in a very bad way, but what can I do? I can't make a living here. As soon as I will earn, I will send you a few dollars"...But I did not believe him that he would send me money. I cried so much that he said to me: "Don't cry and complain. I will go to try something else. I have some compatriots here, maybe they can do something for me."

And he went to his friend, whose name was Goldshteyn. He was peddling junk. He had a beautiful horse and a beautiful cart...It was painted green and white and had such a beautiful harness...Where we lived there was a big yard and a stable where you could keep a horse. I can't forget how beautiful the horse was, with reddish-brown, beautiful fur...He [my husband] brought the horse with the cart to show me and ask if I liked it...And indeed, I liked it...

My husband had no money to buy the horse and cart. Well, what should we do now? My brother Neyte [Note] lent him 75 dollars. He [my husband] went to my sister's husband and asked him to guarantee a "gmiles khsodim" [interest-free loan from the cooperative loan fund] of 50 dollars. But my brother-in-law refused...My husband went to my brother's neighbor named Faynberg and asked to sign a guarantee for 25 dollars. *Faynberg*, a tailor of women's clothing, signed the guarantee.

So, thank God, he could already peddle junk and nuts. It wasn't bad at all. He gave five dollars for the household, however, he lived in Anaheim, fifteen miles from Los Angeles. There was the route to scrap peddling that Goldshteyn had sold him, and there he lived. Over Shabbat he used to come home to Los Angeles with his merchandise...

We couldn't get by on five dollars a week, so

(Page 128)

we argued, he got mad and stopped coming home...My brother also wrote him a letter that he needed the 75 dollars. My husband went into a rage and took his anger out on me and the kids...He went to a lawyer named "Leyens" ["Lyons"], a very smart lawyer...He listened to my husband's complaints. After that, he told my husband to come back on Sunday at three o'clock; and I and also the children should come with him. Lyons sent me a lawyer's summons to come with the children...

My children and I were very frightened. We didn't want to go, but my brother said that we should go very well...The lawyer lived in a small street next to a temple[1], in a very nice house...My husband was waiting for us next to the "kar" [street car] and immediately ran to Gosile, he loved her very much. At that time she was six years old. But she said to him, "Are you off your rocker, and aren't you ashamed to have us called to a lawyer?"

We went to the lawyer's house. He [my husband] presented his complaints. We presented our complaints. The lawyer ruled that he [my husband] must pay us alimony for the two [past] weeks, which is ten dollars, must come home on Shabbat and bring a chicken, and must give us [in the future] six dollars a week for the household.

He [my husband] brought two chickens and gave us six dollars a week for a long time...We still lived on "Feyrmont" [Fairmount] Street...We already had somewhat better furniture. My husband had bought six chairs and two cabinets from a countryman who went back to New York because he couldn't make a living in Los Angeles. He had also bought a table somewhere for a dollar. I painted over the table, and now the table is in fashion, and also the chairs. They are still very nice. It was in 1913, and the furniture is still good even today...This was all when I lived on Fairmount Street with my husband and children...

---

[1] see https://scalar.usc.edu/hc/jewish-histories-boyle-heights/cong-bani-jacob-fairmount-street-shul-2833-fairmount-st

76.

Now I'm going back in time a little bit:

Before my two girls came to Los Angeles, my Libele

(Page 129)

wrote me that she didn't want to come to Los Angeles because she had gone to high school in Paterson and was working after school at a department store where she was making three dollars a week...It was a large department store on North Main Street[1]. The owner, a Jew, was named *Shpits*, and from him she had received work after school and on Shabbat...With this she was able to go to high school and later to college...Mushe also worked a few days a week at Shpits...

I had a family here that I knew from Bialystok, very rich people. They had a big department store with women's stuff, the most expensive coats and dresses. They also made their own hats, the most beautiful and best in all of Los Angeles...why am I writing this? Because it has to do with my Libele and finding work for her. [The family] was called *Tsitrin [Citrin]*.

---

[1] a note by Susan Pasquariella: Libe probably worked at Quackenbush's Department Store at 192 Main Street in Paterson. Quackenbush and his partner Mason sold the store to the Spitzes, who had been in business in Union City. See http://davisullblog.blogspot.com/2008/09/department-store-building-of-week-vol.html and https://allthingsquackenbush.blogspot.com/2019/12/peter-quackenbush-quackenbush-company.html

They also knew my brothers. I had seen her [*Mrs. Tsitrin*] once in Bialystok. I worked with her father and mother in the Preyzman factory. Her father was a weaver, her mother a "shnelerke". I was good friends with her mother and used to spend the evenings with her when all the workers had their evening meal. We used to sit together by the stove and warm ourselves. I saw her daughter when she came to bring dinner to her mother. When she was fourteen years old, she went to visit her uncle in America. The uncle was her mother's brother. Her father's name was *Zalmen*, a tall and handsome man. Her mother was blond and beautiful. Her daughter was also blond and had curly hair. Her mother's name was *Khaye-Leye [Chaye-Leah),* and her family name was *Zilbert*. Khaye-Leye's daughter was the Mrs. Tsitrin...I asked my brother where Mrs. Tsitrin lived. But he told me not to go to her and make a fool of myself...My brother was often visited by Mrs. Tsitirin's brother. I told the latter that I wanted to visit Mrs. Tsitrin and ask her if she could take my Libele into her store. He replied, however, that no one could approach Mrs. Tsitrin.

But I didn't let go of the idea. So I went to her sister-in-law and found out where she [Mrs. Ts.] lived and when you could visit her...She lived in Hollenbeck Park, not far from my brother in Boyle Heights. Apparently she had a yard of houses...

(Page 130)

At ten o'clock in the morning I came to her house and knocked on the door. Mrs. Tsitrin was looking through a small window. She asked me who I was, and I replied that I was the sister of *Neyte Grundens* [Note Grudski] and wanted to ask her a favor...

She called me right in to her house, and I told her that I knew her parents, had worked with them at Preyzman, and was on a first-name basis with them. And I told her that my Libele had written me that she would not come to Los Angeles unless she had a job there...Mrs. Tsitrin told me to write a letter to my Libele right away to come to Los Angeles, because she was going to give her work in her store. And so it really happened...

When my Libele came to Los Angeles, I took her to see Mrs. Tsitrin, and she took a great liking to my daughter and directed her to come to work. She took her into the department that made women's hats...My Libele additionally taught Mrs. Tsitrin's two daughters, one of whom was a cripple...My Libele worked at Mrs. Tsitrin's after school and throughout Shabbat. She paid her four dollars a week...She worked for her for a long time until she finished high school and went to Berkeley, California, to study at college.

77.

I already wrote what kind of apartment we lived in on Fairmount Street...We learned that there was a house for rent on "Kornval" [Cornwell] [1] Street. It was much better than the house where we lived. My Mini[2] went to pay a deposit [for the house]. However, one of our acquaintances also paid a deposit...The house owner didn't know who to rent the house to now. But my Mini went to him and proved to him that we had been the first to make a deposit...However, we had given the deposit right away to the owner, while the other had given it to his brother-in-law...

(Page 131)

we lived, it was far to Brooklyn Avenue. But there, on Brooklyn Avenue, you could buy bread, meat, milk, and anything you wanted in the stores...Cornwell Street was not far from Brooklyn Avenue...

When we got the new house, I don't think anyone was as happy as we were! There had been a fire [in the house] before, so the owner restored the house and painted it. It was really a beautiful house, it was a joy to live there. It was almost like a brand new house and the children livened up...There was already a bathroom there, where you didn't have to prepare extra hot water in the stove and pour it into the tub, and then pour it out again afterwards.

So my daughter "got" the house, and that was a great joy for us...In the house on Fairmount Street, where we lived, it was far to Brooklyn Avenue. But there, on Brooklyn Avenue, you could buy bread, meat, milk, and anything you wanted in the stores...Cornwell Street was not far from Brooklyn Avenue...

---

[1] see https://www.redfin.com/CA/Los-Angeles/318-Cornwell-St-90033/home/6938105

[2] Mini, Minnie= Mushe

When we got the new house, I don't think anyone was as happy as we were! There had been a fire [in the house] before, so the owner restored the house and painted it. It was really a beautiful house, it was a joy to live there. It was almost like a brand new house and the children livened up...There was already a bathroom there, where you didn't have to prepare extra hot water in the stove and pour it into the tub, and then pour it out again afterwards.

The house on Cornwell [Street] was not modern, but by moving from that house to the next, we were virtually going from hell to paradise. The house was four houses from Brooklyn Avenue, so we could already get all the groceries we needed at the stores...It was also conveniently located for going to work. On Fairmount Street we had to walk down the hill to the red street car, and when we came from work we had to walk up the hill. That was very tiring, you could barely manage to crawl up the hill...And one more thing, to get to the street car you had to walk under a bridge and you were always afraid to do so because there were drunks under the bridge. And when we came from work, we were already struck with a great fear...And in the house on Cornwell Street, next to Brooklyn Avenue, the street car stopped right in front of the entrance door.

When we still lived in Fairmount Steet and my Mushe and Libe were already grown-up girls, it happened that they came back late at night from a meeting with friends, and they were so scared when they had to go through Soto Street. Often people would chase them...In those days, Soto Street was not yet built up...

I worked at 448 Spring Street, and it was easier for me now. As soon as I got out of the street car, I could go shopping...When I came back from a hard day's work, I still had to cook dinner for the kids. In view of this, I will never be able to forget what a hard life I led then...

In the new house, the bathroom was as small as a closet; but there was already a [warm water] boiler. If you wanted to take a bath,

(Page 132)

all you needed was a match and there was hot water. However, you could not make a fire, like in a bath stove. And when you sat in the tub in the winter, you cooled off...

The rent was very low...My husband did not live in our house, but in the city of Anaheim. There were the areas where he sold his goods to the farmers, but on Shabbat he always came home, and on Mondays he went back...

78.

The landlord lived in Englewood. One Monday, when my husband had not gone back to Anaheim, but was standing in the yard sorting his merchandise, the landlord came to him about the rent...He said to my husband, "You know what I have to tell you? Until today you paid 15 dollars a month rent, from now on it will cost you 16 dollars a month. And what is to be paid by you in three months, I don't know, because tomorrow I will sell the house." My husband asked, "How much do you want for your house?" He answered, "2800 dollars." My husband asked: "How much is the down payment?" He said, "800 dollars; and the remaining 2000 must be paid off every three months in installments of 75 dollars!" My husband said to him, "I have been living with you for six years. Surely I have privileges over other customers, so sell me your house!"

My husband did not let him go, withdrew from the bank a hundred dollars as deposit and gave it to him...The next morning he went with the owner to the escrow, and gave him an additional 800 dollars; he also paid him 75 dollars every three months. The house had two apartments, one upstairs, one downstairs...My husband rented out the upper floor, where a tenant had already lived before, for 20 dollars a month.

I found out about it when I came home from work and my Gosile came running to meet me and told me that Father had bought

(Page 133)

the house. I was very happy...I also had to sign with my name in escrow as the owner required it...

The children hired a painter and repainted the apartment with the colors they wanted. The two older girls, Mushe and Libe, carried out this work. My little daughter was only ten years old and still had nothing to say...

The kitchen was small and had a pantry with a small window. In the kitchen itself was a large window. We agreed to ask my husband to let us take the pantry out of the kitchen so that it would be bigger and nicer...The pantry only made the kitchen smaller and was so dark with its small window. The pantry was bigger than the whole kitchen. We felt that if we had the pantry taken out and had the small window made into a large window, the kitchen will be very nice and bright with two large windows...

So, together with my children, I asked my husband to have a nice and practical kitchen made for us...It was a very hard thing to get through to him...But we argued until he went to his acquaintance. His acquaintance owned many houses, and he told him what we wanted. The acquaintance said: "If you already have your own house, why shouldn't your wife and children have what they want?" That acquaintance exerted great influence on him, so my husband instructed him to send a carpenter, and everything was really implemented. We had a beautiful kitchen and my husband was even satisfied with it...

Every matter we wanted to change caused us difficulties and we had to discuss with him until he got tired and allowed it...Now, when we had already finished the kitchen and painted the apartment, we thought of having some furniture in the house...But how should we explain it to him? How should we start a conversation with him about it? The kids thought that he was always in Anaheim anyway, so they could buy the furniture and have it delivered home...

There was a fellow countryman, *Mister Miller*, who we went to and bought a couch and two big chairs from. It was leather furniture that was in fashion at the time. My daughter Mushe

(Page 134)

bought them. She bought them on installments...It happened, however, that on the very day Mister Miller was about to carry the furniture in, my husband arrived and started yelling at Mister Miller to take the furniture back because if he didn't he would break every bone in his body... But my children and I stood in between and didn't let it come to a brawl...It was a great shame, because he made such a shout that people came running from the whole block...

79.

Now we already had some presentable furniture in the house and my girls could bring friends to the house...My daughters were acquainted with girls and boys and used to make parties. The leather couch also came in handy because we could use it as a bed to sleep on. It could be pulled apart. And during the day it was a beautiful piece of furniture...We livened up. Only my husband was not satisfied. Nothing pleased him, he was always angry and did not talk to me or to the children...Once he was in a good mood and spoke a few words, there was a happy mood with us...We never knew whether he was doing good or bad business. He used to tell his friends, but never me and the children...That's how almost all my life passed...Always quarreling...And when he was not at home, he gave us little to live on, only six dollars a week. When I was in need of money and protested, he gave me seven dollars a week...I would never have gotten by on those seven dollars a week. But I worked in the coat factory and earned 23 dollars a week. At least when there was enough work. Because several months went by when there was hardly any work, and so I only averaged 11 dollars a week...

A great strike broke out, and *[Benjamin] Schlesinger*[1], who came from New York, enforced that the "feller hands"[2] should receive the same pay here as those in New York. We got more wages then... Two years later, another strike broke out, and the "feller hands" were paid 21 dollars a week. That was the minimum wage. But I got 23 dollars because I was assigned the best work. I did various jobs for the operators and for that I got two dollars more a week than the others... However, I also had to work very hard. Early in the morning I had to make breakfast for the children and prepare dinner, because when I came home from work in the evening, everything had to be ready to cook. It should not take too much time then, because the children were hungry after all. I rushed off so that they wouldn't go hungry or, God forbid, get sick.

---

[1] Benjamin Schlesinger, see
https://en.wikipedia.org/wiki/Benjamin_Schlesinger

[2] "feler hent"= Feller Hands, the persons who have a job that falls under the category of sewing machine operator

(Page 135)

So many sad years passed when there was no peace in the house...My husband used to come home at least for Shabbat, but after our quarrel he often did not even come home for Shabbat. And when he did come, he used to just wash up and run to the restaurant to eat...This was the worst punishment for us...I saw how many families lived in domestic harmony, only with us was such a misfortune...

And yet I was neither a fool nor a jinx! But I could not live peacefully with my husband...The children were already grown-up girls and were also annoyed by him. But this led to even more hostility. He assigned all the blame to me for inciting the children against him so that they should not love him...However, I just wanted the children to get along well with him so that he would feel more attached to our home. But it was no use. The children saw how hard I worked all week, washing and ironing clothes on Sunday, so that they would have clean clothes all week...And they were dressed cleaner than the children of the mothers who didn't work in the factory...

I envied my neighbors, for whom Sunday was the most beautiful day. They put on nice clothes and went out with their husbands and children. I sent my girls off to do something on their own, and my husband preened himself and went out alone...My heart felt like bursting with pain and anger.

80.

My Libele was already 18 years old. She had graduated from high school and was preparing to go to college in Berkeley...The

(Page 136)

morning she had to leave, my husband was in the yard sorting things. I didn't want her to leave without saying goodbye to her father. He would only get more upset...My daughter Libele was very angry with him and didn't want to go into the yard to say goodbye to him. But I took her by the arm, led her to her father, and she shook his hand. He was very pleased...He instructed her to wait, went in the house and gave her 25 dollars...

It had already become quiet in the parlor...He was already behaving better to me and the children. He also went to his acquaintances and boasted that his daughter had gone to study at Berkeley college.

Three months later, in 1920, the flu broke out and many people died. There was not a single house where no person was sick. My husband was in Anaheim, the flu was raging there too. He was scared and came home. My Gosile was eleven years old at the time and caught the disease in a neighbor's house...When she got sick, I stopped going to work. Shortly after, I also got sick, as did my older daughter Mini, who got a high fever...He himself [my husband] was also very sick. But he dragged himself around the house to take care of the children...

Among our acquaintances was a doctor, and when he came to us and found us all sick together, he sent a nurse to take care of us all...I was very sick and had a high fever. I remember how I had to vomit constantly...The nurse kept handing me black coffee, always a spoonful of black coffee, and she saved me...I was already feeling better, and so was my husband, so he sent the nurse away...Mini [Mushe], however, became very ill and got pneumonia. My husband ran to Doctor *Dzheykobs [Jacobs]* in the middle of the night and brought him to Mini...The doctor instructed us to have her taken to the hospital right away...but we didn't have money to pay for the hospital after all. So my husband told the doctor that he would give him the truck he was peddling with. But the doctor said that we would see later...In the meantime, Mini could no longer breathe and

(Page 137)

stuck out her tongue... The doctor called the hospital, it was two o'clock in the night. When she [Mini] was already in the hospital, they put her in a box under a machine that produced steam. They put hot linen cloths around her and saved her...

And hear what happened the next day. My Libele was at Berkeley college after all. She had heard what the newspapers were saying about Los Angeles, that the flu was raging there and many people were dying. And she left her college where she was studying and told them [the officials] she was going home. She came home immediately with a mask on her face. When I saw her, I didn't recognize her. She was wearing one of those white coats that the nurses wore. She said that she had felt something had happened at home...She immediately went to the French hospital[1] to visit Mini. Mini was already ablte to speak again...

81.

My Mini was in the hospital for six days. Doctor Jacobs had arranged that we didn't have to pay much, no more than 44 dollars. It would have actually cost three times as much...Doctor Jacobs was very good to us...He was our family doctor and took very little remuneration...

My husband was completely changed, he was very happy that we all stayed alive. He was already no longer going to Anaheim but peddling more nearby. ...Every day he came home with his goods and gave us 15 dollars a week for the household. When the situation calmed down, he peddled again in Anaheim. There he could earn more. The farmers sold him the pipes of the oil wells. There was copper in the pipes, and that brought all the profit. But he really worked very hard, and he was not a strong man. I also worked very hard. I wanted my children to be able to study...

My Libele learned very well at Berkeley. During the first year she worked after college with a rich family. She looked

(Page 138)

after their children. When she had studied one year and came to me during her vacations, she said that it was very difficult for her to work after school. She would not be able to do her homework in the long run...The first year cost me 450 dollars. I told her to continue with the college, I would try to help her...

---

[1] see:
https://en.wikipedia.org/wiki/File:French_Hospital,_Los_Angeles,_California,_1909.jpg and https://www.latimes.com/local/lanow/la-me-chinatown-hospital-closes-20171218-story.html

When she came home for the vacations, she left the very next day to work. She earned three hundred dollars during the vacations. I had already saved up the excess money...The other two years already cost 750 dollars each...When she went away to study, we made sure she had about 500 dollars, and we sent the rest of the money to her later. She never had too much money, but she knew how to live frugally...

She studied medicine for three years in Berkeley and after that she studied in New Orleans. In New Orleans one year cost 1150 dollars, and the third year 1250 dollars. In the third year she had to study for the "state license", and therefore it cost more.

God helped, and she was able to fulfill her wish. She finished her studies as a doctor. The doctors there wanted to give her 150 dollars a month, but she didn't want to stay in New Orleans and came home to me...And just imagine my great joy...After all, I had worked for her to achieve what she wanted...For that, no work in the factory and in the house was too hard for me; the main thing was that she achieved what was good for her...I wore old clothes and let my children go in newly sewn clothes...

I was talking my daughter Libele into a lot of courage, because when she went to the college, you had to learn on dead people, and she already wanted to run away. I wrote to her that she should strengthen herself and pull herself together. Now she would still have to learn on dead people, but later she would be able to learn on living people and bring much benefit to the people. I also wrote to her that a good doctor could do much good for people. And that I hoped she would also become a good doctor and be able to do good for people...She wrote to me that she would follow me; and she actually listened to me and did not regret it.

(Page 139)

82.

When she arrived from New Orleans, she had already completed her medical studies as a doctor for children. However, she had to practice at the hospital in San Francisco for one more year. After that year, she came to Los Angeles and worked at a children's hospital in Hollywood. She also worked there for a year and then opened an "office". However, she did not have many patients and had to maintain the office, apart from her living expenses. [Anyway,] there were doctors who performed surgeries. They called for her to perform anesthesia on their patients, and she was paid well for that. This way she could keep the office and additionally have enough for her own needs.

When she had to open her office, she went to my sister to borrow 300 dollars. My sister, however, referred her to her husband, and her husband said he wasn't a bank. ...My brother Neyte, may he rest in peace, gave her 300 dollars. He also lent her the rent for the first month, it was a hundred dollars a month. The second month my daughter Libe could already pay with her own money...

She was not yet known in the city, so she still had some difficulties, but that did not last long. Her office was next to another office, that of a dentist. He was still a youthful, unmarried man and a young doctor, but he was more successful than my Libe. He had a large, rich family. All his friends came to see him, and his friends recommended him to their friends...This dentist was once visited by the head doctor of the Board of Health (the city's health department) to have his teeth treated. He told the dentist that he needed a pediatrician in his office. In response, the dentist told him that he had a pediatrician for him, a woman. The dentist's name was *Lesly Shvoder*. The dentist immediately called my daughter in, and the head doctor liked her, so he hired her right away with a high salary. He soon sent her through the schools to the small towns. She didn't have a car yet and borrowed

(Page 140)

600 dollars from a friend so she could buy a car, I think it was a "Dodge". That was 28 years ago, 1924...

83.

The Board of Health sent her to examine the children of the poor farmers who were studying in the schools...My daughter told me that the poor farmers had no cooking stoves, so they cooked outside in the yard. The mothers did not bathe their children for a whole week. My daughter issued a decree that the mothers should bathe the children more often and make sure their heads were clean...She also saw to it that the school administration made sure that the children who had nothing for lunch got something to eat.....

My daughter took really good care of the children and was therefore liked by everyone she looked after...But she worked very hard, having to drive around in the cold and rain in winter and in the heat in summer. She left home very early in the morning, and came back home late in the evening. She had to travel very far, but was satisfied that she had her living and was already a good doctor...And she never abandoned her mother. She gave me fifty dollars every month...She was very good to me and no one was as lucky as I was...I thanked God every day for helping me and I had joy with my Libe...

Well, you can tear yourself apart as much as you want, but if you are not blessed with "mazl" [luck], nothing helps. While I was at work, I was not at home all day...My Gosile, already 13 years old, used to practice the piano when she came home from school...I had bought her a piano, and my brother's son also came to my house after school, he was about 11 years old...Since my brother Neyte had a grocery, and his wife Flore also came to the store to help him, their boy usually came to us after school. We lived on the same street, not far from each other. My little girl practiced the piano every day. I already wrote that my husband [had started] peddling in Los Angeles, so he came home every evening...

(Page 141)

One evening when he came home he was very irritable and worn out...He couldn't stand the way my little daughter was playing the piano and my nephew was singing along to it...He was a very hot tempered person and yelled at the kids...I don't know exactly how it happened, but it escalated into a big fight between him and the kids...He ran to the phone and wanted to call my brother. But my Gosile wouldn't let him complain about the boy...When I got home, I didn't meet him [my husband]...My girl was in so much worry, she said to me, "I am so sorry for what happened, because he has a headache all the time. But believe me, it wasn't my fault"...

And once again he was angry with me and accused me of not teaching the children to love him. But it was not my fault. He was constantly walking around in a bad mood and angry. That's why the children were always annoyed with him...The children went to their girlfriends and saw how nicely their fathers talked to their children and how cheerful it was at their homes, how father and mother were always in a happy mood, and the father went out together with the mother to spend time; there the children would also have respect...

My children liked to bring their girlfriends and acquaintances home and also to leave to stay with others in the house. But that alone brought misunderstandings, and war could break out at any moment. This affected me. When I went to work in the morning, I was cheerful, and when I came home, disaster awaited me...

It did not heal up anymore; he did not want to reconcile. He stopped giving us the fifteen dollars a week...I told him that if he didn't want to give money, he wouldn't get food anymore. He then grabbed me to hit me. My Mini saw that he was hitting me and stood up for me. She scratched his face...Well, you can already imagine that we had to run out of the house. If we hadn't run out of the house, the biggest disaster would have happened. I pushed Mini through the window, we ran to a neighbor and waited until he left the house. But with that, our whole life was also destroyed...

(Page 142)

84.

He went to a lawyer and filed a divorce suit against me. We were already in our sixties then. A small wound had become such a big one, because it was never healed. I regret that even today, and yet twenty-nine years have passed since then. But still the pain tears my heart...

He had stored a lot of iron on the yard, which he was now selling. He moved to Anaheim. I sent my Mini to visit him every few weeks. And if I didn't send her once, she also went to visit her father by herself...When she came to see him, he was happy. He was very fond of Mini who had received her name after his mother...

I forgot to tell you that even before he moved away from us, he had my daughter Libe, the doctor, called to him. When she came, he told her that her opinion would decide how he would behave, but she was angry with him and told him to leave if he wanted to move out...After that, he complained to his acquaintances that his daughter, the doctor, told him to move out of the house. Therefore, he was moving out and would never come home again...

I was lamenting and crying so much. I ran to my brother Neyte, to the grocery on "Kort Gas" [Cord Ave]. At that time, also my brother Shie [Ishye] was in the store. He had come from New York and was working in the store with Neyte. I was complaining to my brothers about my suffering, and that I couldn't stand it...And just as I was talking to my brothers, a call came that there was another scandal in our house. Immediately Neyte went to my house and just managed to calm my husband, who had argued with my Gosile.

A few days later, my husband called my brother Neyte, saying he wanted to talk to him and Ishye, and wanted to meet them at a compatriot's house called *Falti [Waldy?]*. My brothers actually came to the compatriot, only my husband did not come...If he had come, we might have reconciled...

Now, as I write this, it is 1954, and the accident happened in 1925...So my life passed in sorrow...Everyone

(Page 143)

who will read my lines can surely imagine the sufferings I went through then...Who can fully put all this into words... After all, you are still ashamed to tell what you feel deep in your heart... A good friend has no joy in it, and an enemy pays you back and gossips about you on top of it...

Such worries and problems have accompanied me on my way...But God gives the remedy for such plagues. My daughter Libele was already working in the "Board of Health", she lived with me and gave me fifty dollars every month...

85.

I have already written that my husband bought a house and had to pay the [previous] owner 25 dollars every three months. There were still 300 dollars to pay for the house...Six months passed and the man who had sold the house came to me to collect his money...He said that my husband was no longer paying for the house. But in the meantime, he had found out what had happened to us and told me, "I could take the house away from you, since your husband has not paid everything. But I will not sin..." The [previous] owner was a very fine person, a gentile who lived in Inglewood.

My daughter Libele had saved 75 dollars, and I had also saved 75 dollars, so we brought the gentile the money...When we came back from Inglewood, we drove on another road. On both sides of the road it went down deep, like into a pit. The road was being repaired there. We got lost on the narrow road, though, and my daughter had to reverse her car for a couple of miles. We were very scared, because my daughter had learned to drive only a short time before...I still remember what a great fear my daughter and I had until we found the right way...

That was a long time ago. Today, when I describe it, I am 86 years old...They were such bad times, and yet

(Page 144)

I survived them...Because, if God wills, He gives man the strength to get over all sorrows...They say that you can't live on any joy and you can't die from any sorrow...and that is really true. On the contrary, the more sorrow I went through, the stronger I became...I think God has given me enough strength to endure so much and to take care of my children. For a while they were not well, they were sick all the time.

Six months later, after I was in Inglewood with my Libele, we paid the remaining 150 dollars, and our house was debt-free.

My husband, who bought the house, had to stay in a small room or garage in Anaheim at an old gentile's home. I never went there. When I sent my Mini to tell him to reconcile and come home, he said he would not. He was making good money there peddling iron and nuts and other various things. And when Mini came home from Anaheim, my heart was torn with sorrow because he had to stay there in a small room or a garage in a foreign country. Even now, as I write this story, my heart cries inside me...

86.

There in Anaheim, he got very sick and got cancer. He came to Los Angeles and called to tell me that the doctor had told him he was sick and not allowed to work. So he hadn't worked for a while, but he hadn't gotten better, so now he was going to Kaspare-Cohn Hospital[1]...The Kaspare-Cohn Hospital was on Seventh Street, next to Whittier Boulevard, which is the street where you go to the cemetery to lay a deceased person to rest ["khesed-shel-emes"][2]...Now there is a small park where the hospital was, and in place of Kaspare-Cohn Hospital is now Cedars of Lebanon Hospital in Hollywood. He told us that he will call us again as well as he will be admitted there. The next day he called to say that he was already at the hospital. When my Mini visited him, he informed her that the doctor told him,

(Page 145)

he had to have surgery and something had to be taken out through his neck, there was a growth there. He did not want anyone to come for the operation and did not say when the operation would be performed...Later, when my daughters and I came to visit him, he chased us out...We went home, but I sent Mini to visit him every evening. I told her to tell him that he was welcome if he wanted to come home, as if nothing had ever happened and I would take care of him. However, he said that he had good friends who took care of him...

---

[1] see https://www.jmaw.org/kaspare-cohn-los-angeles/ and https://scalar.usc.edu/hc/tuberculosis-exhibit/movetoboyleheights and https://www.jmaw.org/cedars-sinai-jewish-los-angeles/ and https://en.wikipedia.org/wiki/Cedars-Sinai_Medical_Center

[2] khesed-shel-emes or Chesed-Shel-Emeth: a) The commandment to escort a deceased person to his or her final resting place, b) Name of the Chevra Chesed Shel Emeth (Jewish Free Burial Society) in LA, who founded Los Angeles' first Jewish cemetery https://scalar.usc.edu/hc/jewish-histories-boyle-heights/home-of-peace-memorial-park-and-jewish-cemeteries-in-east-los-angeles

His good friends brought a lawyer named *Lanson*. He knew the whole story. His good friends told the lawyer that he had a two-story house and that one half should be given to the hospital for the terminally ill and that he should be cared for there as long as he lived. He [my husband] said that he would think about it...

It was before Rosh Hashanah, and the wife of one of his comrades, a [deceased] compatriot of the small town, Brok, went to her husband's grave. When she returned from the cemetery, she went to the hospital to visit him [my husband]. She told him, "You have a family and a good wife, they will take care of you even more as in the hospital for terminally ill people. Don't sign over anything to anyone except your wife and children."

The next day he called my brother Neyte saying that he wanted to come home and that my daughter Libele should pick him up...My daughter Libele actually went to him and brought him home...I went up to him and gave him my hand. I made his bed and my Libele instructed me to put a feather bed under his one side because he was so thin, just skin and bones...I remember my Libele crying and telling me that the doctors had told her that he had cancer...

Even before he left home, he had been sick. Doctor Jacobs had ordered his teeth pulled, if not, he would get cancer. In fact, he had his teeth pulled then, but it looks like it didn't help..

(Page 146)

87.

I took good care of him and he was very happy. I know he called his good friends and told them: "I am back in my own home." It was Rosh Hashanah and the friends who returned from the synagogue came to visit him. The synagogue was next to our house...

I wanted to give up my job to take good care of him, but he wouldn't let me. My older daughter also wanted to give up work, but he did not want this either...Early in the morning I prepared cream of wheat for him for breakfast every day and for lunch I cooked some chicken soup for him. He couldn't eat much, just suck out a bone...He lived on the little bit of soup and sucking out bones, unfortunately he could not swallow food...

The mattresses on the beds were hard and worn. Across the street, on Brooklyn Avenue, was a large mattress store. He took me to buy three mattresses. I asked, "why are you buying three mattresses?" and he replied that it was not opportune to buy one mattress for himself, but not for the others...However, it was me who paid for the mattresses, not him. I remember when the wife of his late compatriot paid him a visit and I told her about the mattresses...She said to me, "Oh dear, I am sorry to say that man is so foolish and stingy and does not realize how sick he is". The woman was Mrs. *Boodne*, she was the wife of his best comrade and good friend, who had been dead for eleven months...

There was just a grocery on North Soto Street to buy, and he said to me that he would buy the grocery and our lives would be easier. But man proposes, God disposes. He had been at home just three months when he got worse. The doctor said he needed another operation. He was operated on, but this time he was very bad...They took him home, he was very weak. He could not swallow at all, unfortunately. Above his shoulders, red "pasn" [stripes, streaks]

(Page 147)

had formed on him, like a cock's comb...He could no longer urinate...

My brother Neyte took him to Kaspare-Cohn Hospital, but they would not admit him there. They would have had to register beforehand, and since he hadn't registered beforehand, he couldn't get a bed. He had to be taken home...

My daughter Libe was engaged at the time to a dentist, a very good man. He came to us with my daughter Libele and told us not to worry, he would watch all night...He put hot water bottles on him all night and was lying next to him on a small sofa...

My husband noticed how good his daughter's fiancé was to him and took out his gold pocket watch early in the morning. He said to him, "I give you this watch as a souvenir of me. I am very pleased that my daughter Libele is getting such a good groom". The dentist actually accepted the golden watch and wore it for a long time...

88.

[At some point] we could no longer keep my husband at home. He needed special treatments that we could not do at home...Doctor Jacobs, who was Mister Boodne's son-in-law, came and was able to get a bed for my husband at Lincoln Hospital[1] on Soto Street near Sixth Street...But they couldn't save him anymore...We visited him every day. Sometimes he wanted to see us, and sometimes he sent word for us to go again...

I forgot to write that the second time he was brought out of the hospital, my brother Neyte asked him if he wanted to talk about his life. But he said that he had not had a good life with me. My brother then asked him why he had not divorced me? He replied that he had once filed for divorce, but immediately regretted it because he did not want

(Page 148)

me to marry for the second time and the children to have a stepfather.

At Lincoln Hospital he was in agony and it was heartbreaking to watch...After he had been at Lincoln Hospital for only a short time and I came to visit him with my daughter Mini, he said to me, "Quick, call your brother Neyte!" My brother came, and he said to him: "I want to do something for your sister, she is a good woman, I must take care of her so that she will no longer have to toil in the factories. Go and get a public notary." [2]

---

[1] see https://www.pinterest.com/pin/801500064930041084/

[2] According to family lore, Rachel said the following about it: "At that moment I thought to myself if only he had said that long ago. My life would have been sweet, not bitter."

My brother brought a public notary and [my husband] instructed him to write that he bequeaths the money he owns as well as the house to me, his wife. My brother Neyte asked, "And what are you transferring to your daughters?" He replied: "One dollar each." My brother then said that such a will was not really a worthy thing if he had only one dollar written down, and caused 100 dollars to be written down for each daughter...

He died [in 1928] at Lincoln Hospital, 560 Soto Street...

He wanted us to arrange a beautiful funeral, and we did. It cost me 500 dollars...300 dollars I gave to my children. He left 1500 dollars. The truck we sold for 140 dollars. We couldn't live on the rental income [of the upper floor] because at those times the apartment was often empty...And when we had a little bit of rental income, we had to do repairs all the time. So this was rather a bad business. [1] We were also often sick and I had to toil, I still had to work in the factory...

89.

After my husband died, my brother used to go with me to the cemetery to see my husband's grave. He would then put flowers on his grave, because my brother loved flowers very much...My brother and I used to go to my husband's grave every Sunday.

(Page 149)

My older daughter Mini and I went three times a week until we had a tombstone put up...

As I wrote before, I continued to work in the factory where I had already worked for 14 years...

---

[1] literally, "iz avek di khale far der hamoytse": the challah bread had already disappeared even before the blessing over the bread was spoken

Eleven months later it happened that my brother Neyte died...Even when my husband was alive, my brother had always complained to him that he suffered from heartburn and severe headaches...I still remember how my husband answered him that it had started like that with him too...It was indeed the same disease, also cancer...My brother Neyte, may he rest in peace, did not want to admit that he was also so sick...

My brother Neyte was the best person, he was so good to me and my children. Whenever I was in need, he helped me...And when after 11 months such a sad stroke of fate hit me, that my husband and my dear brother died, I almost went crazy...My brother only lived to be 49 years old...We lived on the same street, not far from each other. The street is called Cornwell. Even today I live on Cornwell...My brother left his wife, Flore, and three sons...The oldest was named Louie, he went to college; the second was called Moyshe [1], he was 16 years old and went to high school. The third was named Samele [2], he was 11 years old and went to public school.

What a grief it was in our house and at my sister-in-law's with her children...I still remember how my brother's wife stood with her children at the open grave and did not want to leave. The younger boy, Sam, cried even more than anyone else, he was only 11 years old after all. My brother Neyte died in 1929, and now, as I write, it is already 1955...

The greatest sorrow was to look at my old mother. She was 85 years old at the time and might have lived to be 100, but the death of her son shortened her life...She was a very pious woman and comforted herself

by saying that one must not go against God and sin [by criticizing and questioning His works]. But she just couldn't forget her son...He was very good to her. He had a grocery.

_____

[1] Given family lore he was also called "Shepsele"

[2] Given family lore he was also called "Mischa

(Page 150)

He used to work very hard, but he never forgot his mother. Late at night, when he went home, he put milk, butter, cheese, eggs and other things at her door...After the death of her son, my mother was sickly all thbe time and lived another 5 years...She was very pious and used to do many good works ["mitsvot")...As soon as she had knowledge of a sick family, she tried to help...She went to the bakers and butchers to receive challah and meat and bring it in to the poor families, and she even left them some money...This is what supported her the last five years she lived...

She was used to her son bringing her food, and when he no longer did so, she began to skimp and be stingy and became as skinny as a skeleton...She didn't have to cut back so much, because before Neyte underwent the operation he had signed over a thousand dollars to her, and his wife Flore brought her twelve dollars every month. Sheyne Gitl also supported her. She lived with me, and she didn't lack for nothing, but she wanted to accumulate money, and she actually saved up money and wrote [1] a Torah scroll for the Cornwell "Beith David" synagogue...

---

[1] According to family lore, she did not write the Torah scroll herself, but ordered it.

90.

When my brother Neyte passed away, he left a policy of 25,000 dollars and even smaller policies...He sold his grocery for 12,000 dollars before he died. He left several properties and owned a lot of land in the mountains. He was a good businessman and could make money out of anything he touched. He also had stock for several thousand dollars...He owned a property in Beverly Hills. His wife sold the stock and built a large building on the property. It now has the value of 45,000 dollars...Before he passed away, there was a plot of land [on sale] on 84th Street. The owner of the property could not find work, and my brother bought the property from him along with a part owner, his name was *Gadef*. This was a month

(Page 151)

before his death. A person does not anticipate what may be in store for him...A few months after my brother's death, my sister-in-law built a four-story house together with Mr. Gadef; Mr. Gadef was a builder...

My sister-in-law Flora [Flore] was a talented and smart woman. She was rich, and she was a good mother to her three sons. My sister-in-law Flora was also an honest and beautiful woman. She never had anything to do with other men; she only took care of her children. After the death of her husband, she lived another 24 years. For 16 of those years she was healthy, but for eight years she was very sick...She had high blood pressure and didn't pay attention to it...She was so beautiful that no one thought she could be a sick person...She had still prepared dinner for herself. She had come to my house in the evening to have dinner. She asked me to give her some carrots and green peas. She preferred not to eat from the dinner I had prepared because of her illness. So I ran to buy her carrots and green peas, and she made herself another dinner... That was the last time she ate dinner in my house...She had come that evening for a business affair. At that time she was already living in Beverly Hills. She owned a house on Soto Street. She had asked my daughter Mini to go to a real estate agent and turn him the house over for sale. She [Flore] wanted 7000 dollars for the house...My Mini found a customer for her who was ready to pay 8500 dollars. She [Flore] was surprised with joy, but she regretted it right away because real estate agent didn't want to pay my Mini the commission over 100 dollars...My sister-in-law got totally enraged with the man from the real estate. She was so upset that her pen fell out of her hand while she was writing a document that only my Mini can sell her house...She took a few steps through the house and collapsed...

We laid her down on the sofa. Her son Moyshe was also with her. Flore had suffered a stroke at that time and was paralyzed on the right side of her body, affecting her head, one arm and one leg. She also could no longer speak...

(Page 152)

We immediately called the other two sons, Leyen [Louie, Lion] and Sam. A doctor was brought. She [Flore] didn't know what was happening to her anymore...She was taken to the County Hospital. She stayed there for a week, and she got better. She was taken in a convalescence home, and when I went to visit her, she could already walk around on a cane, what a joy that was!

She was brought home, and in the house she used to walk around with a cane. However, she became ill a second time and was hospitalized again. She then got better, but after that it got worse again...

Once a day a black woman came to clean the house. She didn't like the way the woman cleaned the house, so she wanted to sit with her to give her instructions, but she fell down and lost her speech. At this point, she had already been paralyzed on one side for four years, but could still speak and tell where she was in pain...Unfortunately, she had to struggle for eight years before she died. It is now one year and eight months after her death. May her soul shine brightly in the Garden of Eden.

91.

Two years ago, I thought that I could write down my life story after all, and I actually began to write. Acquaintances of mine read [the first pages] and encouraged me, so I wrote about a hundred pages. But my youngest daughter got sick. She was sick for a very long time, so who could still think about writing. I didn't continue writing for over six months until she got better. And when she was healthier, I started writing more and wrote another four hundred pages. When I was already counting on being able to finish my life story, I had to stop again, because I started to restore my house, which was in very neglected condition. My neighbor, who had lived in the house for nine years, had moved out and his apartment was in such a state of disrepair that it was simply not possible to rent it out anymore...I had thought that it would be best to re-plaster the two apartments, downstairs and upstairs [1]. In addition to plastering

the house, we also had new stairs made, new plumbing and new electrical wiring installed, had the roof redone and repainted the house. It took a year. I had to watch out for the carpenter. Every day I was on my feet from eight o'clock in the morning until five o'clock in the evening, everyone had to be watched out for, the carpenter, the plumber, the electrician, the painter, the roofer...My daughters were annoyed with me because I had initiated all this...But now I don't have to worry anymore; no one recognizes that this was an old house. Anyone who comes and looks at the house can't believe it. My daughters are happy, and when I go into the yard, I beam with joy.

(Page 153)

I had started to restore the house in the month of Kheshvan [October, November], and it lasted until the Kheshvan of the year 1955...And by the time I had stopped writing for a year, I had forgotten all about it...Old people find it hard to remember. When I stopped writing a year ago, I was 87 years old, and today I am already 88 years old. Thank God I can still manage so well...

Now I will describe to you how the purchase of the house next to me came about. This second house belonged to a man named *Savel*, and when he and his wife passed away, his children wanted to sell the house to us because we were good neighbors. They talked us into buying it, saying it was a bargain. They asked for 2200 dollars.

---

[1] According to family lore, Rachel commented in addition: " The exterior was constructed of wood, which I did not like. I covered the wood with stucco. I also added one room to each flat and enlarged the front porches. I installed a new staircase of white terrazzo like material called diato, and replaced the wooden banisters with black wrought-iron banisters."

92.

In the third house from us lived a neighbor named *Elman*. I asked him if the house was worth 2200...And do you know what he did to me? Next to Elman was the Cornwell shul, the Beyt-David synagogue. So he just went to the shames (synagogue servant), took 20 dollars commission from him, and went with him to the children of our deceased neighbors. And the shames bought the house...

The shames who bought the house was called Mister Zepe. He told my daughter that he would sell me the house if I paid him a profit of 300 dollars on top of the purchase price...I refused.

(Page 154)

Mister Zepe rented the house to a peddler of chickens, roosters and nuts. He hired women to crack nuts for him. My daughter Mini and I cracked nuts too...But the neighbors all around revolted because the chickens were crowing all night. They went to the Board of Health and caused the peddler to move out. Mister Zepe couldn't rent the house to anyone else because it was very run down...He wanted to sell me the house for 2500, but I didn't want to.

In the meantime, however, I learned that he found another peddler who wanted to buy the house from him, offering him 2800 dollars. And this peddler also peddled chickens and roosters. The former peddler, who traded with chickens and roosters, could be forced to move out, because it was not his house. But, if the new peddler bought the house, he could not be forced out. So I had to buy the house and paid my "rebe gelt" [1], namely 650 dollars more...Mister Zepe rented the house from me and paid 25 dollars a month for it...When we bought the house, it was 1937, and in 1938 we restored it a little bit, because I wasn't happy with the way it looked.

----

[1] "batsoln rebe gelt"= to pay dearly

In 1942, we were thinking about what we could do with the two-story house we owned and the one we bought in addition to it. There were 4 garages at the back of the single house. We had them torn down and moved the two-story house to where the garages had been. The house that we bought in addition[1], we moved a little bit over to us, but it was damaged in the process, and on top of that, the plaster in our two-story house fell down...We had to have all the rooms upstairs and downstairs re-plastered and also had a new floor laid. We had the house painted inside and out and added a nice porch. It cost about $5,000...

That was in 1942, when I was 72 years old. Now, while I am writing, I am already 87 years old and a year ago, as I wrote, I remodeled the two-story house...We made a big mistake when we moved the two-story house in 1942. The lot where the house once stood remained

empty. It has been like this for 14 years and it seems that the devil himself prevented us from doing anything. Since the Korean War, building has become more and more expensive. I had already drawn up a plan to build on the empty lot, but nothing came of it until now. [2]

_____

[1] According to family lore, Rachel used to say, " I had dreamed of building a four unit apartment house on that lot so that I could have something to leave to my children. But I was not able to do it. I had even hired an architect to draw up a plan but nothing came of it."

[2] the single house

(Page 155)

Maybe I'm completely crazy to worry so much about the property, which has been vacant for 14 years...But maybe I'm still better off than those who have to look for a room; especially since people don't like to rent to persons who are too old...Those already have to prepare to go to a retirement home, but it is not easy to get in there. And if you are already accepted there, you are not satisfied. They [the residents] would quarrel with each other, because unfortunately old people are irritable. The different needs don't fit together...You don't get out of the old people's home alive...

If you talk to the old people in the old people's home, they say, what is the use of all this life, if you can't get back your youth and you are old and exhausted and sick to boot. They [others] think that old people are senile. I know this from myself. It seemed to me that I am still as mentally awake as before, but I see how the children say that I don't know anything anymore. And you have to admit that they, the children, are right...Of the elderly, people think that "old" equates to "cold."...

93.

Why am I writing about old people? I have a brother, Yehoshue [Ishye] Velvel, who is in a nursing home. Five years ago he came to visit us. He said that he would be able to visit us again three years later...However, he was not completely healthy five years ago either, and now he is sick all the time and unfortunately had to go to a nursing home...I am not healthy either, so I cannot go to see him in Paterson, New Jersey. I have not received a single letter from him in which he does not complain and cry that he is in a home for old people...

He has four children, three sons and a daughter, who pay 150 dollars a month for him for the old people's home. He complains that the people

(Page 156)

there don't treat him well. [At least], he has the best food, a nice room and good conditions...He has a good doctor and he asked him when he could leave the nursing home to go to Los Angeles? He is not happy about being confined to one place. Now that he has raised four children, he can't be with any of them. They would rather pay as much money as they can, but not have their father or mother with them. This is very upsetting to him, and that's why he is so depressed...He can't get used to the people who live with him...When there are two or three in a room, one wants to sleep, the other wants to read or do completely different things. So it comes to a big quarrel between them...

He writes such tearful letters and says that he needs to get it off his chest. My brother is already eighty-five years old and sick, and if he can tell the people close to him what hurts him, it makes his heart a little lighter...My brother was a fine and educated young man. When he was younger, he taught the Gemara and writing, and he was such a handsome man...When he was, I think, around 22 or 23 years old, he was already married. In Bialystok there was a workers' uprising, and Ishye was a socialist at that time [1]...In Bialystok, young boys from other cities arrived and caused all the factory workers to go out on strike... For the factory owners, this meant a fierce war with the workers...And since my brother was a weaver of cloth, he became "a redner" [an orator] and agitated the weavers in his speeches to go out on strike...

In Bialystok there was a large forest, the "Zverinitser" [Zwierzyniec] forest, and one Shabbat evening all the weavers of the factories gathered there and discussed about going on strike...They chose my brother to be the leader of the strike.

However, there were many spies in the forest, and among them was one from our colony named Ofrim [Efraim]. Efraim was a foreman in Bialystok. He told the factory owners

---

[1] For the reader who is more deeply interested in the revolutionary workers' movements in the Krynki and Bialystok area, I highly recommend reading the book "As It Happened Yesterday" by Yosl Cohen. My English translation is available both in book form and on the JewishGen website,

https://www.jewishgen.org/yizkor/Krynki2/Krynki2.html

(Page 157)

that he knew who had incited the weavers to go on strike. In the middle of the night, gendarmes and the police came and took him [my brother] to prison. At that time, he had married not long ago. His wife, Rokhl, was pregnant with their first child. The child, a daughter named Enye [Anye][1], has already married off her own children today.

The prison was on Wasilkowska Street, which was also called "Unter der Turme" [Behind the Prison]. I, my mother and brothers and my sister-in-law Rokhl, also lived on " Unter der Turme", five houses away from the prison...We hired advocates, but they could do nothing. The spy Efraim did not even justify himself to our family...My brother was in Bialystok prison for three months and then he was transferred to Grodno prison. He remained there for six months. When he came back from Grodno prison, he was "swollen like a mountain"...After he served the time in prison, he was exiled to a foreign city, Kherson. There was no weaving mill there, so he learned to iron men's shirts. This was not a job that could support a family...He worked hard, but could not make a living. In Kherson he did not live in freedom either. He was kept there on "volnye poshelenye", in America they say on "parole". If during the "volnye poshelenye" one transgressed a law, it was very bad. One was sent to Siberia. The police were very watchful of him.

94.

My brother, his wife and child struggled a lot for a little bit of living. His wife supported him a bit by earning some money and helped him to iron the shirts. She also cooked for acquaintances...

Now, after the two and a half years [parole] were up, he didn't know where to go...In Bialystok it would have been hard for him to get work anywhere, because all the factory owners knew his name...

---

[1] She was also called "Chana"

My brother's wife's sister lived in Krynki. Her name was *Rashe-Kayle.* She brought her sister Rokhl [Rachel] with her

(Page 158)

three children to Krynki and my brother went to London...In London he waited until my two brothers in Paterson sent him a ship ticket...My two brothers, Neyte and Alter, they shall rest in Gan Eden, were very good people, not only good to my brother, but to everyone...When my brother was in London waiting for the ship ticket to America, he had nothing to eat. So he sold his things, even his talis [prayer shawl] and tefillin. At that time he was already a free thinker.

When my brother Ishye came to America, he went to Paterson, to my brothers. He got work there as a weaver. After two years, he sent ship tickets to Krynki to his wife and three children...

I haven't even written half of what my brother suffered in Russia. I'm not even talking about his time in prison, but about how he was still working as a weaver in Bialystok...The workers used to start their work at six o'clock in the morning, when it was still dark, and come home at ten o'clock at night, sometimes not until midnight...On Thursdays they usually stayed overnight at the factory, and on Friday they worked a full day, and then went home in the evening. From Thursday morning to Friday evening, the employees worked without stopping...If a weaver still got a bad warp, he was to be pitied. He lay with his whole body on the loom.

Young people had arrived from Warsaw, Vilnius and other cities, studying in the universities and enlightening the workers about their situation; it became a revolt. Those young people who came from the other cities were called revolutionaries. A battle to the death began. The workers used to be banished to the prisons...The workers, who had been enlightened, organized themselves. They consulted with each other and took all the workers from the factories to strike, not only the weavers, but also the girls, the spoolers, the "warpers" and the "nuperkes"...The workers were very satisfied that their eyes had been opened and they had been shown the way to a more luminous world.

(Page 159)

And if a factory owner did not want to agree and settle the strike, they would send him a letter saying that he would regret it...And you think that didn't scare them? Yes it did, many factory owners were afraid and settled the strike, but many refused. They were ambushed in side streets and beaten until they agreed with the workers...Other factory owners preferred to spend the money not on slightly better pay for the workers, but on the police to be protected by them...

The prisons were full... If an informer wanted to slander someone as a revolutionary, his statement was enough for [his victim] to be sent to Siberia or to forced labor.

That was in 1896, and my brother Ishye Velvel was then a young man of 23 years. Now he is 85 years old, an old man, and I write all of this because of him. Whenever I get a letter from him, he cries and complains of his bitter fortune of being in a home for old people. He complains about his sons, because when they come to visit him and he cries in front of them, they ask him: "Were you better off in Bialystok prison?" He would answer that he was better off there than he is now as an old man in a nursing home... He is writing this to me in order to get it off his chest.

95.

Since I have written before that the workers gathered in Bialystok, I will describe what happened to a girl. Across the street from the house where I lived, there lived a mother with four children, two adult girls and two boys. The girl's father was in America and had already taken the older girl to live with him. After that he wanted to bring his other children and his wife. They had already sent their luggage ahead and were to leave for America a few days later. On Shabbat evening, it was customary to gather in the Zwierzyniec wood, so the girl went to the forest. She wanted to say goodbye to all her comrades and friends with whom she had worked in the factory. She

(Page 160)

also wanted to say farewell to the forest, knowing that she would not be coming back to Bialystok anytime soon.

She was an 18-year-old girl, tall and very pretty. But because she was so tall, she was also seen more than anyone else... On that Shabbat evening there was a big meeting. The workers were enjoying themselves and held a big demonstration. They carried red flags and shouted, "Down with the Tsar!"

There was a joyful mood, because a few weeks earlier on "Khanaykes" [Chanajki, district in Bialystok] they had killed the governor. He was a very bad person. He had put many workers in jails, and for that they had put him out of the way. No one was caught [in the action]; many workers were arrested, but they could not be proven guilty and they all had to be released...For this reason, the meeting with the flags took place. And because the girl was so tall, they gave her the red flag to carry.

But [suddenly,] many policemen and gendarmes came running into the forest and took hundreds of workers into custody. The policemen trampled on the people; a bloodbath took place in the forest. The girl fled home and hid there in a small chamber...At night, policemen and gendarmes came, dragged the girl out of her chamber and locked her up in the prison.

Regrettably, now the mother and her children could not go to her husband in America...the mother was crying and lamenting a lot. The father sent hundreds [dollars] from America, but it was not possible to free his daughter. The girl was in prison for two years. She was even supposed to be transferred to the Grodno prison, but, after paying a lot of money, she remained in the Bialystok prison.

96.

I just remembered that I haven't written anything about the spinning mills yet...

The wool from the sheep was usually taken to the spinning mills, where it was washed by machines in a cauldron. After the washing process, the wool had to be dried, which was done by machines driven by steam...When the raw wool was selected, washed and dried, it was dyed.

(Page 161)

The wool was dyed in the "farbanye" [the dyeing factory]. For this purpose, it had to pass through a large cauldron of dye, so that the colors would hold up...At the cauldron stood people who had no specialized qualifications, and who therefore had to work for only three rubles a week...They used to work twelve hours a day. As I wrote, my father also worked in the dyeing factory.

When the wool was ready to be dyed, it was given to brushing so that it became like absorbent cotton. For this purpose, there were brushing machines that softened the wool. These machines were also powered by steam.

As soon as the wool had softened on the brushing machines, strands of thread were made from it. These strands were wound up and then removed from the machines. They were put together in bales ["shroymen"] and packed in boxes. After that, they were formed into bundles, and from the bundles, the "spoolers" wound bobbins.

The bobbins came to the warpers who prepared the warp yarn tapes, and the warps came to the weavers...

Christian girls, mostly Polish but also Russian, worked in the spinning mills. They worked for two rubles a week. Jewish girls were not allowed in the spinning mills...There were Christian girls and Christian masters...Also in the spinning mills you had to work 12 hours a day...

The Christian girls went to work barefoot and carried their shoes in their hands. They were dressed in linen skirts and jackets made of chintz...They worked for very little money...Labor leaders who had come from other cities had worked very hard until they were taught to demand more money for their work...

The spinners were in the majority and didn't get paid much either...There were thousands of workers in the spinning mills...A spinning mill had three stories, sometimes even four or five. And the building was maybe 500 feet long...

And when the workers were gaining, already earning a little more and working fewer hours, the factory owners were in fact not giving away any more at all. Because when they paid more, they earned more on their goods at the same time [by increasing the price], and became even richer...

(Page 162)

Not only the weavers and spinners went on strike, but also the carpenters, the turners, the blacksmiths, the people in the offices, and the merchant's clerks in the stores...

97.

Not far from Bialystok was a small town, Supresle [Supraśl]. It was a German town, where only rich Germans lived...The Germans owned the biggest factories in Supraśl, which were powered by steam. There, in Supraśl, the Germans had the best woven silk. Both the silk and linen and "kortn" [cheap cloth] for low-cost men's and children's suits also had to be woven by steam-powered machines, as well as women's dresses...

The labor leaders began to organize the workers in the Supraśl factories as well...However, it was difficult to implement and took a lot of time to finally take the workers from the Supraśl factories as well, which were built like fortresses and had closed, heavy gates all around.

Those who organized the strike risked their lives. They depended on the German workers not to betray them. Sometimes, when they met honest workers, they succeeded, but sometimes they met workers without a sense of responsibility. Thus, many fell victim to the damned German traitors...

It had already become quieter, the factory owners had gotten used to paying their employees a little more, and employees and employers already had a friendlier relationship. Between them had never been a good friendship, but the situation was already better than before...

But just when things had become a little more bearable for the workers, the great disaster of 1914 broke out - the war. The Germans had invaded Russia. They took Bialystok and confiscated all the Jewish factories. All the rich factory owners unfortunately became so poor that they barely managed to escape to America to peddle socks... At that time they regretted that they had not appreciated their workers and given them enough wages for a decent life...

(Page 163)

It was such a tragic war; so much blood was shed by the inhabitants...It lasted a long time, I think four years...The Germans took Warsaw, Bialystok, Vilnius and other cities and towns, such as Sokółka, Krynki, Amdur, Kuznetse [Kushnytsia] and Grodno...

Why am I writing this? Because they also captured our colony...The Germans destroyed not only our colony, but also our local cemetery, where my father, my brothers who died young, my grandpa, my grandma, my uncles, my cousins, acquaintances and good friends were buried...

May all their souls shine brightly in Gan Eden...

Epilogue

[not part of the original book)

My mother completed writing her memoirs at the age of eighty eight. She lived for almost twenty years after that, active and alert, interested in the world around her, reading the Forward every night until midnight, never missing any of the television newscasts, eager to discuss world affairs with any of her friends and relatives who came to visit her.

And every Shabbes, without fail, she attended the Synagogue until the last few years of her life.

At the age of ninety she realized her dream to erect a four flat building on the vacant lot next to her home. She had also begun a sequel to her memoirs about her life in Los Angeles. She continued to write until she was one hundred and three. She died in December, 1974 at the age of one hundred and seven.

In the words so frequently used by her throughout her memoirs, "May her soul shine brightly in Gan Eden".

Gertrude "Gussie" Reed

List of Names

[This list is not part of the original book. It is incomplete and based on the knowledge at the time of publication. The page numbers provided refer to pages in the original book.]

Name	Relationships, Notes	Page (first reference)
Kositza, Rokhl-[H]ene or Rachel-Anna, born Grutski	Author, eldest daughter of Leybe and XXX Grutski, died with 107 years on Dec.16, 1974	
Grutski, Abraham	Grandfather of the author. He came from Zubritz with his first wife Rachel.	5
Grutski, Rokhl [Rachel]	Wife of Abraham Grutski, mother of Leybe Grutski	11
Grutski, Blumke	First daughter of Abraham Grutski and his first wife	5
Grutski, Gitl	Second daughter of Abraham Grutski and his first wife	5
Grutski, Sheyne	Third daughter of Abraham Grutski and his first wife	5
Grutski, Motl Shmuel	First son of Abraham Grutski and his first wife	5
Grutski [Grutske], Leybe [Leybke, Leybeshke]	Father of the author, second son of Abraham Grutski and his first wife. He was born in 1844 and died in 1893	5
Grutski, Mendl	Third son of Abraham Grutski and his first wife	5
Grutski, XXX	Second wife of Abraham Grutski	6

Grutski, Artsik [Artshik]	Son of Abraham Grutski and his second wife	6
Grutski, Yerakhmiel [Rakhmiel, Rachmil]	Son of Abraham Grutski and his second wife, later worked in a field, made soap	6
Dubrovski, Yeshue	The author's great-grandfather	7
Grutski, XXX	The author's mother. She came from Grodno	10
XXX	Twin sister of the author's mother, settled in Katerinodar	7
Dvoyre's [Deborah's], Khone	Uncle of the twin sister of the author's mother	10
Velvel the Bezdetnik [the Childless]	One of the uncles of Rachel's mother	10
Khaye [Chaia] Feyge	Aunt of Rachel's mother	10
Rive-Leye	First girl of Khaye-Feyge	10
Teybl	Second girl of Khaye-Feyge	10
Zeliks, Khaye	Girl in the colony, related to Leybe Grutski, married a man from Krynki	11
Zeliks, Moyshe	Brother of Khaye Zeliks	11
Grutski, Yehoshue Velvel [Ishye, Shie]	First brother of the author	13

Grutski, Abraham-Berl	Second brother of the author	14
Grutski, Mendl	Third brother of the author	14
Grutski, Yakev-Moyshe [Jacob-Moshe, Alter]	Fourth brother of the author	14
Grutski, Note [Neyte, Notke, later called Israel Grundens or Grodzky or Grodesky]	Fifth brother of the author	14
Grutski, Sheyne Gitl [Gosye]	First sister of the author	14
Grutski, Simkhe-Berl	Sixth brother of the author	14
Leyzer, Dovid	Baker in the colony	31
Peshe Leye	Second wife of Dovid Leyzer	31
Avrohem [Abraham] Itse	Son of Dovid Leyzer with his first wife	31
Libe	Daughter of Peshe Leye with her first husband	31
Tsirl [Zirl]	Daughter of Libe and Avrohem Itse, the author's friend	31
Khaye [Chaia] Feygl	Second daughter of Libe and Avrohem Itse	31
Shmuel Yankl	Son of Libe and Avrohem Itse, elder brother of Khaye Feygl	31
Mordekhay Moyshe [Mordechai Moshe]	Son of Libe and Avrohem Itse	31

Khaye-Peshe [Peshe-Leye, "di bobe"]	She helped the women to give birth	32
Libe	Daughter of Khaye-Peshe who became a kind of midwife after her mother's death	32
Etke's, Yehoshua	Neighbor of the author in Bialystok, named after his mother Etke	33
Saraste, Arke [alias Aharon or H. Suraski]	Biggest factory owner in Bialystok at that time, prominent Chasid	33
Leye	Old woman who owned a [kind of] restaurant in Bialystok	37
Khaye [Chaia] Tamara	Daughter of Yehoshua Etke's [from her father's first marriage], worked in Leye's restaurant in Bialystok	37
Kinze's, Moyshe [Moshe]	Man from the same colony, later a weaver in Bialystok	38
Nekhome	Wife of Moyshe Kinze's	38
Doctor Prage	Eminent doctor in Bialystok	38
Yaner's, Efraim Itsi	Son of Itsi Yaner's, a weaver	39
Sokher [Sokher-Arye]	Man from Adeslk	40
Rabbi Shmuel	Father of Sokher, a great Jewish scholar	40
Peshe	Wife of Rabbi Shmuel, she ran a bakery	40

Khayke di Teperke [Chaike the Potter]	Woman who traded in Adelsk	42
Shoshke Merke	Old, blind woman in Adelsk	42
Zundl	Owner of a huge store in Adelsk	43
Mekhlye [Mechlie]	Wife of Zundl	44
Khayim [Chaim] Hershl	Zundl's older son	44
Efraim Leyke	XXX	44
Gershon	Sokher's son	44
Abe's, Kalman	Blacksmith in Bialystok, came from the same colony	45
Reyzke	Kalman's wife	45
Moyshe Khayim [Moshe Chaim]	Son of Khaye the Potter, cabinetmaker	45
Rokhl [Rachel] Itke	Daughter of Velvel Leyzer, the author's friend, married Moyshe Khayim	45
Velvel Leyzer	Brother of Khayke the Potter's husband, a village tailor	45
Yakev [Jacok]-Shiye	Older Boy of Velvel Leyzer, a tailor	45
Moyshe [Moshe] Shiye	Baker in Adelsk	52
Peshe	Girl from Bialystok, the author's friend, a spooler	55
Preyzman	Very big manufactorer in Bialystok	55

Endler, Leyzer	Manufacturer in Bialystok	55
Khatseles, Yude	Foreman of Preyzman	57
Avrohem [Abraham]-Berl	Cousin of the author's mother, a water-carrier	57
Peshe	Avrahom Berl's beautiful and kind-hearted wife	57
Yehoshue [Ishye]	Third brother of Avrohem Berl, a bricklayer	57
Tseyteles, Avrohem [Abraham]	Weaver, a foreman or master in a Bialystok factory	58
Leyzer, Dovid	Old man in the colony	60
Itsi Yankel and Rokhl [Rachel] Itsi Yankel's	Couple in Bialystok who rented the author a room	65
Dina and Berl	Itsi Yankel's and his wife's daughter with her husband, a plumber	65
Sheyne Bashke and Yisroel	Itsi Yankel and his wife's second daughter with her groom, a dressmaker	65
Dreyne	Itsi Yankel and his wife's third daughter who worked together with the author in Leyzer Endler's factory	65
Kositza, Avrom Itskhok [Abraham Itzchok]	The author's husband, his father's name was Aharon, he came from Brok, which is next to Tshizeve [Czyżew-Osada]	66
Meyer der Royter [Meier the Red] and Leye	Couple in the colony	69

Itsi's, Dovid	Foreman in Preyzman's weaving mill	69
Sore and Tsivye	Two sisters, related to the author by marriage	70
Feygl	Sister of Sore and Tsivye, was married by Leybe's stepbrother, Rakhmiel	70
Kroler, Mendl and Mindl	Farmer and his wife, parents of Sore, Tsivye and Mindl	70
Alte	Friend of the author in Bialystok	71
Libke	The author's cousin	72
Yoel	Young man who fell in love with the author, he came from Adelsk	72
Henekh the Feldsher	Yoel's father	72
Kositza, Moyshe [Moshe] Mendl	Brother of the author's husband	74
Brukh, Moyshe [Moshe]	Rich man and factory owner in Bialystok, son-in-law of Arke Saraste	74
Shmulek	Weaver, Master in Preyzman's factory	77
Kositza, Sheyne Khaye [Chaia]	Avrom Itskhok's sister	78
Preyzman, Hinde	Wife of the factory owner Preyzman in Bialystok	79
Belakh	Brother of Hinde Preyzman	79
Kositza, Mushe [Mushele, Mini, Minnie]	First Daughter of Rachel and Avrom Itskhok	82

Sokher and Shloyme	Avrom Itskhok's uncle and his son	83
The Gorush ["The Divorced"]	Nickname of one of Avrom Itskhok's uncles	83
Khaye and Isroel	Sokher's blind daughter and her husband	83
Kositza, Libe [Libele, alias Snyder, Lillian]	Second daughter of Rachel and Avrom Itskhok [1899 – 1991]	90
Grutski, Leyzer Meyer	Cousin of the author	91
Grutski, Motl Shmuel	Uncle of the author	91
Leyzer the Red	Father of an acquaintance in the colony	93
Leyzer's, Meyer	Son of Leyzer the Red	93
Kroyne	Daughter of Rachel's landlady in Bialystok	94
Grutski [?], Yisroel Khayim [Israel Chaim]	One of the author's cousins	95
Fayvl	Husband of Rivke Rokhl [Rachel]	96
Grutski [?], Rivke Rachel	One of the author's cousins, from the same colony	96
Leybe the Vashelkover [Vashlikover]	Weaver in Bialystok	97
Grutski, Sore [Sara]	Wife of the author's brother Alter	100
Grutski, Luie [Louie, Lion or Leib]	Older son of the author's brother Alter	100

Shmuel	Master in Preyzman's factory, Preyzman's nephew	101
Mikhl [Michel]	New master and supervisor in Preyzman's factory	102
Lapiduses	Rich family who had a cloth factory in Bialystok	103
Shloymke the Feldsher	Feldsher who worked in the hospital and was killed during the pogrom of 1905	103
Leye	Pious Woman in Bialystok	104
Doctor Kazanovitsh	Doctor in Bialystok	108
Grutski, Rachel	Wife of Ishye, the author's sister-in-law	112
Zalmen	A lodger	113
Kositza, Gosi [Gosile, Gosyele, Gussie, alias Gertrude Reed]	Third daughter of Rachel Kositza. [G. died in 1979]	113
Finklshteyn [Finkelstein]	Silk Manufacturer	115
Daymant [Diamant]	Associate of Mr. Finklshteyn	115
Grutski, Flore [Flora, Faiga]	Wife of Notke, the author's brother	118
Haywood the Great [William Dudley]	Leader of the Industrial Workers of the World	119
Flynn, Beth [Elizabeth Gurley Flynn]	Leader of the Industrial Workers of the World	119
Grutski, Louie	First son of Notke and Flore	120

Grutski, Moyshe [Misha]	Second son of Notke and Flore	120
Lize	Wife of the owner of a cloak factory in LA	121
Miler [Miller], Eyde [Ida]	Friend of the author's sister-in-law	121
Goldberg	Name of a couple who rented the author a room	122
Doctor Bless	Doctor in LA	122
Sachs, Morris	Factory Owner	123
Katsop	Factory owner- together with Morris Sachs	123
Goldshteyn [Goldstein]	Friend of the author's husband	127
Faynberg [Feinberg]	Note's neighbour	127
Leyens [Lyons]	Lawyer	128
Shpits [Spitz]	Owner of a large department store in Paterson	129
Tsitrin [Citrin]	Name of a rich family who had a large department store in LA	129
Zilbert, Khaye-Leye (Chaia-Leah) and her father Zalmen	Khaye-Leyes daughter was Mrs. Tsitrin [Citrin]	129
Miller, Mr.	Fellow countryman	133
Schlesinger, Benjamin	American Trade Union offical	134
Doctor Dzheykobs	Doctor in LA, son-in-law of	136

[Jacobs]	Mr. Boodne	
Shvoder, Lesly	Dentist, neighbor of Libe (Lillian)	139
Falti [Waldy?]	Compatriot	142
Lanson	Lawyer	145
Boodne [Budne], Mr. and Mrs.	A good friend and his wife	146
Grutski, Sam [Samele, Shepsele]	Youngest boy of Note	149
Gadef, Mr.	Builder	151
Savil [Savel], Max	Owner of a house at Cornwell Street	153
Elman [Eluk Elmore]	The author's neighbour	153
Zepe, Mr.	Shames	153
Efraim	Informer	156
Enye [Anye, Chana]	Granddaughter of Ishye Velvel	157
Rashe-Kayle	Sister of the wife of the author's brother	158

www.ingramcontent.com/pod-product-compliance
Lightning Source LLC
Chambersburg PA
CBHW060338100426
42812CB00003B/1045